The Best of
Daily
Wisdom
for Women

The Best of
Daily
Wisdom
for Women

CAROL LYNN
FITZPATRICK

BARBOUR
PUBLISHING

Published by Barbour Publishing, Inc., P.O. Box 719, Uhrichsville, Ohio
44683, www.barbourbooks.com

*Our mission is to publish and distribute inspirational products offering
exceptional value and biblical encouragement to the masses.*

Member of the
Evangelical Christian
Publishers Association

Printed in the United States of America.

ℐNTRODUCTION

In Christ alone we find the wisdom we seek:

But by His doing you are in Christ Jesus, who became to us wisdom from God, and righteousness and sanctification, and redemption, so that, just as it is written, "Let him who boasts, boast in the Lord."
1 CORINTHIANS 1:30–31

Since its first release in 1997, *Daily Wisdom for Women* has become a perennial favorite, with sales topping three-quarters of a million copies. Now, for the first time, editors have chosen their favorite readings from this bestselling devotional to create this brand-new "best of" edition. May this beautiful collection encourage your heart as you seek the true wisdom found only in God's Word.

Be blessed!

In the Garden

*When the woman saw that the tree was good for food,
and that it was a delight to the eyes, and that the tree was
desirable to make one wise, she took from its fruit and ate;
and she gave also to her husband with her, and he ate.*
GENESIS 3:6

On a day she'd never forget, Eve stood beside the "tree of the knowledge of good and evil" and began listening to the seductive voice of the crafty serpent. How could she know that this voice desired to entice her and Adam away from God and the security of the Garden of Eden? She innocently chose to ignore the truth of God's Word and obey that new voice.

And Adam, who loved her, listened to her voice. He then accepted her invitation to join her in partaking of the fruit of the tree. As a result, cloaked with garment skins of animals sacrificed to cover their sin, Adam and Eve were forced out of this physical garden paradise. Yet the echo of God's loving promise lingered in their ears. . .a Redeemer would come.

Thousands of years later, Jesus returned to another garden, choosing it as His place of prayer. Kneeling there, He would accomplish for men and women this task of abiding in the Father and obeying His commands. And on the cross the sacrifice of His life provided forgiveness, once again allowing access to God's presence. . .now within a spiritual garden of prayer.

*Lord, I know I have walked away from You at some
point of sin. That's why You sent Jesus to be my Savior.
Forgive me, and enable me with Your strength to run
from sin and toward prayer.*

Seeking Wisdom

To receive instruction in wise behavior, Righteousness, justice and equity; To give prudence to the naive, To the youth knowledge and discretion, a wise man will hear and increase in learning, And a man of understanding will acquire wise counsel, To understand a proverb and a figure, The words of the wise and their riddles.
PROVERBS 1:3–6

When asked by God what he wished for, Solomon answered, "Wisdom." Looking back over your life, if you'd been afforded this same opportunity in your early twenties, what would your response have been?

Like most of us, at that age wisdom probably wasn't high on your priority list. Instead of asking God or your parents for direction, you more likely turned to your peers.

Natalie, a strikingly beautiful girl who'd just turned seventeen, found the advances of an older man extremely difficult to resist. Disregarding all the precepts she'd learned from years of Sunday school, Natalie turned instead to a non-Christian girlfriend for advice. "Go for it!" the friend encouraged with gusto.

A decade later that friend has been married and divorced. Natalie herself found out too late that her "boyfriend" already had a wife and baby.

Satan may be out of the garden but he still finds his way into vulnerable areas of our lives. But God is with you, even in times of sinful temptation. He's promised to give you the power to withstand such moral crises.

Lord, surround me with friends who know You and Your Word. Surround me in a crisis so I can still hear Your voice of wisdom and reason.

Fishers of Men

"Come, follow Me," Jesus said,
"and I will make you fishers of men."
MATTHEW 4:19 NIV

Walking beside the glistening blue waters of the Sea of Galilee, Jesus saw two brothers casting their fishing nets. When He spoke the words recorded above, Peter and Andrew must have been intrigued. But Jesus didn't invent the phrase "fishers of men." Philosophers and teachers of that day used this term to describe those who captured men's minds.

The passage goes on to say that Peter and Andrew immediately left their nets and followed Jesus. But this wasn't their first invitation to follow Him. They had gone with Jesus to Capernaum and Galilee and later returned to their trade of fishing. However, this particular invitation was to full-time ministry and they responded wholeheartedly.

But why did Christ want these fishermen? Peter and Andrew were men of action who knew how to get a job done without quitting or complaining. Their tenacity would be an asset to Christ's ministry, of soul winning.

Jesus came not only to save but to teach men and women how to have true servants' heart. The substance of ministry is service. When the apostles agreed to follow Christ, they accepted the call on His terms, not theirs.

Lord, show me clearly where I can be of service within my local body of believers. Perhaps there's a small hand in the Sunday school just waiting to be held.

Vocalizing a Prayer

*And when you are praying, do not use meaningless
repetition, as the Gentiles do, for they suppose that
they will be heard for their many words.*
MATTHEW 6:7

Remember kneeling beside your bed and praying
when you were a kid? Why did it all seem so simple
then? We just talked to God like He was really there
and kept our requests short and simple.

Then, as you got older, the lengthy and spiritual prayers of the "older saints" became intimidating.
So, where's the balance? Reading a little further in
this passage from Matthew, at verse 9, Jesus gives us
His own example for prayer. If you can remember the
acrostic ACTS, you'll have an excellent formula for
prayer: Adoration, Confession, Thanksgiving, and
Supplication.

As we come before the Lord we first need to honor
Him as Creator, Master, Savior, and Lord. Reflect on
who He is and praise Him. And because we're human
we need to confess and repent of our daily sins. Following this we should be in a mode of thanksgiving.
Finally, our prayer requests should be upheld. My
usual order for requests is self, family members, and
life's pressing issues. Keeping a prayer journal allows
for a written record of God's answers.

Your prayers certainly don't have to be elaborate
or polished. God does not judge your way with words.
He knows your heart. He wants to hear from You.

*Lord, Your Word says that my prayers rise up to heaven
like incense from the earth. Remind me daily to send a
sweet savor Your way!*

Turn Your Ear to Wisdom

*For the Lord gives wisdom; From His mouth come
knowledge and understanding. He stores up sound
wisdom for the upright; He is a shield to those who
walk in integrity, Guarding the paths of justice,
And He preserves the way of His godly ones.*
PROVERBS 2:6–8

Every family has at least one relative who cannot get
his act together. (Meanwhile the rest of us scratch our
heads and wonder how he can miss the obvious, every
single time.) It's as though these people have to fall in
every pothole in the street because it never occurs to
them to go down a different road.

Are you smiling yet? Is someone in particular
coming clearly into focus? Now, hold that thought.

God's Word says wisdom is truly a gift since it
comes from the mouth of God, from the very words
He speaks. And all God's Words have been written
down for us, through the inspiration of the Holy
Spirit. Therefore, those who refuse to accept God's
guidance, who refuse to ask for His wisdom—those
hapless relatives, perhaps—will never see the light of
reality.

Know that if you hold fast to the precepts contained in the Bible, you will walk in integrity. Instead
of gravitating toward potholes, your feet will be planted
on the straight and narrow road.

*Lord, I can't change my relatives but I can change myself.
So, if my head is the one peeking out of the pothole,
please pull me out!*

FALSE PROPHETS

"Beware of the false prophets, who come to you in sheep's clothing, but inwardly are ravenous wolves. You will know them by their fruits. Grapes are not gathered from thorn bushes, nor figs from thistles, are they?"
MATTHEW 7:15–16

While working within a Christian cult awareness ministry—a real barometer of what's happening in present-day society —I began to wonder about a person's ability to discern truth.

Perhaps the authors of the letters I read just went about the process backward. Those seeking answers tend to try everything, like sampling dishes at a buffet brunch, and then choosing which to accept and to reject. The main problem with this approach is that life only affords us so much time. What if you run out of time before you find the one thing that does work? Pretty risky, isn't it?

That's why God gave us a way to recognize the true teachers from the "wolves." "You will know them by their fruits," scripture says. Those who abide in Christ preach the message that is consistent with the one Christ Himself taught. That salvation comes to us by the grace of God and is obtained through the belief that Christ's blood shed on Calvary's cross, has cleansed us from our sin.

Don't be afraid to ask questions. True teachers will always be pleased to give straightforward answers.

Lord, there are so many voices. Please help us to hear Yours, so that we won't be led astray by the wolves in sheep's clothing, who make a mockery out of Your great sacrifice for us.

A Furious Storm

*When He got into the boat, His disciples followed Him.
And behold, there arose a great storm in the sea, so that
the boat was covered with the waves; but He Himself
was asleep. And they came to Him, and woke Him,
saying, "Save us, Lord; we are perishing!"*
MATTHEW 8:23–25

One evening my husband and I attended a meeting for Adult Children of Alcoholics. This particular group was for Christians, who shared hope and inspiration from the Scriptures. We read verses on a certain subject and then attempted to derive strength from principles we could then apply to our lives.

When we read this Scripture, the Lord reminded me of some previous difficulties I'd encountered. The disciples were in the midst of a storm, just as I had been. Yet Jesus was with them in the boat. They woke Him, in the throes of panic, sure that the waves would swallow them up. Many times in the past I succumbed to this same degree of pandemonium, sure there was no way out or through the problem.

With sudden clarity I understood this passage. Jesus took the disciples to the height of the storm's raging fury, yet all the time He was with them. Later on in this chapter Jesus rose up and rebuked the winds and sea and everything became perfectly calm. Yes, the storms of life will attempt to ravage me but Christ is there, amid the frenzy, ready to deliver by just the power of His Word. He will carry me safely to the other side of the shore.

Lord, keep my eyes focused not on the storms of life, but on Your incredible power to deliver me from them.

King Forever and Ever

The Lord is King forever and ever;
Nations have perished from His land.
Psalm 10:16

When my sisters and I were young we lived in a huge, newly built, custom home. My father's pride and joy, as a part-time carpenter, was the gleaming oak staircase going to the upstairs.

One day several of us got into a fight over who should have control of a bottle of india ink. As one sister attempted to carry the glass container downstairs for a parental pronouncement, another sister knocked it from her hands. The bottle crashed down the stairway, its thick black ink cascading furiously all the way to the first floor.

My father looked as if he were going to have a stroke when he saw the mess. During the next few years he tried everything to eradicate those angry stains but nothing would take them away, short of rebuilding the entire staircase.

Satan, whose dominion is the world, has devoted all his efforts to eradicating Christianity. Yet, while the evil one's influence can seem as ugly as any ink stain, Satan's mark on this earth will not be permanent. The reason? God's Son, Jesus Christ, lives forever within those who call upon His name. And despite the efforts of the evil one, Jesus will remain King and will one day soon come back to claim this earth for His own, forever and ever.

Are you assured of your place in Christ's kingdom?

Lord, as this world becomes increasingly evil, reflecting the one who holds its "title deed," remind me that You're coming back to claim all that is rightfully Yours.

Who Are the Faithful?

Help, Lord, for the godly man ceases to be,
For the faithful disappear from among the sons of men.
They speak falsehood to one another; With flattering
lips and with a double heart they speak.
Psalm 12:1–2

Who are the faithful? They are the ones who continue to follow God, no matter what obstacles are thrown in their path. One of the faithful, a dear friend who has debilitating multiple sclerosis, is one of the most joyful Christians I know. Jo must be assisted to the podium, but once seated on a wooden stool the weakness in her legs is forgotten. The songs which emanate from her wondrous spirit are a radiant tribute to her Savior, Jesus Christ.

Another friend, Sue, has led a Bible study for years, despite the fact that her husband is frequently out of work and their finances are at times nearly nonexistent. She continues at her post, knowing that God is not out of resources. And each time their family stands on the brink of impending disaster, God rescues them.

By now you have probably decided that it doesn't pay to become one of my friends. But I must reassure you that neither of these women consider shrinking back from following Christ. Instead, they agree with the apostle Paul, that these present circumstances and trials are but "light and momentary" compared with the peace we will have in Christ for all eternity.

Lord, I have watched people carry burdens that humanly speaking should be unbearable. Yet with these trials You give them incredible joy. I praise You for all You are!

A GREAT LIGHT

The people who walk in darkness Will see a great light;
Those who live in a dark land,
The light will shine on them.
ISAIAH 9:2

Shortly after four o'clock in the morning, the students at California State University at Northridge awoke at the jolt of an upward-thrusting earthquake. Forced into blackened hallways, they groped along the walls, attempting to locate the exit doors from their dormitory buildings. Thick clouds of plaster dust, shaken loose from the interior walls, had filled the air, making it impossible to see. But escaping their physical confines did not bring them into the light. The sun had not yet risen and massive power outages had shut down all outdoor lighting. Only the first murky rays of daylight could expose the extensive destruction to the area.

Like the students of this university, the Israelites had no idea that such a great depth of darkness had overtaken them until they were in the midst of it. God previously had provided them with great light, for He communicated directly with their leaders. But the Israelites chose to act as though the switch of truth had never been turned on. They were caught up in the dark snare of idolatry.

Are you refusing to act on God's insight, insisting on pursuits that distract you from worshiping Him? How we spend our time is but a habit, and habits can be changed, by repatterning our actions. Walk in the light, as your Father intended.

Lord, change the desire of my heart to seek and know You better. Take my life and use me for Your purposes.

Our Advocate and Defender

*"Therefore everyone who confesses Me before men,
I will also confess him before My Father who is in heaven.
But whoever denies Me before men, I will also deny him
before My Father who is in heaven."*
MATTHEW 10:32–33

My sisters and I attended private schools for most of our lives, but that did not render us immune to rowdies or bullies. And since we walked a few miles to school each day, we were at times easy prey.

Busy with friends her own age, my older sister didn't usually accompany my younger sister and me on our morning trek.

However, when we returned home one day relating that two big kids from the nearby public school had threatened to beat us up the next day, she rallied to the cause. As she instructed, we traversed our normal route while she lagged watchfully a short distance behind.

Suddenly the two boys jumped out of the bushes ahead. And just like a superwoman, our sister pounced on them, easily overpowering both and giving them bloody noses in the process. I'll never forget that scene as long as I live. It felt so incredible to have an invincible defender!

If we know Jesus Christ and have responded to His invitation to receive Him as Savior, Jesus remains forever our advocate before the Father, saying with love, "She's mine." Know that you are so precious to Jesus that He gave His life for you. Doesn't it feel incredible to have Jesus as your defender?

Lord, how reassuring it is to know You mightily defend not only my body but my soul against attack.

17

JOSEPH HONORS GOD

Now Joseph was well-built and handsome, and after a
while his master's wife took notice of Joseph and said,
"Come to bed with me!" But he refused.
GENESIS 39:6–8 NIV

Perhaps you remember this account from Sunday
school, as it's often used to reinforce God's expectation of purity. A young woman told me the other day
that in the nineties the notion of celibacy before marriage is definitely passé. But for Joseph the very future
of Israel teetered on his decision.

Joseph could neither dishonor Potiphar, an
Egyptian officer of the Pharaoh, nor disobey his God.
But day after day Potiphar's wife kept after Joseph,
hoping to wear down his resistance. Can't you just
picture this "thirty-something" woman, doused with
perfume and decked out in the latest sheer fabrics,
grasping Joseph's biceps? But when Joseph's outer garment falls away as he flees, she proceeds to act like a
scorned woman and has Joseph thrown into jail.

But God had a plan. Through an incredible chain
of events Joseph is found innocent and released from
prison after he correctly interprets the king's disturb-
ing dream. Eventually Joseph's position is restored and
he creates a stockpile of grain that sees both Egypt
and Joseph's restored family through a great famine—
the one he had predicted in that dream.

Joseph's moral stand preserved the very ancestral
line leading up to Jesus Christ.

Lord, I can't look ahead to see how a critical moment
of obedience fits into Your overall plan. Please give
me Your strength when my human desires threaten to
overpower me.

Why Jesus Spoke in Parables

And the disciples came and said to Him,
"Why do You speak to them in parables?"
MATTHEW 13:10

Jesus' main purpose in coming to earth was to communicate God's love by His perfect words and actions. Certainly He could clearly articulate a point when He desired. So why did He shroud many of His teachings behind a veil of curious stories?

Jesus Himself explains: "'Therefore I speak to them in parables; because while seeing they do not see, and while hearing they do not hear, nor do they understand'" (Matthew 13:13). Who was Jesus talking about? Only moments before He'd been conversing with the scribes and Pharisees. And although they had great knowledge of God's Word, they refused to see its very fulfillment before their eyes. Everything Jesus did and said confirmed that He was their long-awaited Messiah. Yet they closed their eyes and stopped up their ears.

Then Jesus spoke to the great multitude that had followed Him to the seashore. How well He knew that just because they followed didn't mean they desired to hear His message or respond in faith. Therefore, He spoke in parables, or words of truth hidden under an imaginary net. Only with the hand of faith could these followers lift a corner of the net and view the truth.

Yet to those whom He knew would respond, He provided plain words. How open have you been to God's Word?

Lord, Your truth surrounds me. Please lift my eyelids to see it and stir my heart to respond to Your Word.

19

Rescued from My Enemies

He reached down from on high and took hold of me;
he drew me out of deep waters. He rescued me from my
powerful enemy, from my foes, who were too strong for
me. They confronted me in the day of my disaster,
but the LORD was my support.
PSALM 18:16–18 NIV

David wrote this psalm at a time when he was being pursued by Saul. Imagine David's terror as he and his band of loyal followers clung within the concealing walls of caves for shelter while Saul sought to slaughter him. During this time of desperation, David learned to lean on God's power, convinced in his heart that He alone could rescue him from harm.

Have you ever known such desperation? A time when even the ground beneath you seemed unable to support you? Perhaps you were exactly where God wanted you, just as David was, and yet untold trials and tribulations were heaped on you anyway. Did you doubt God's presence? Did you realize that He could act in your behalf, despite the obvious circumstances?

The very nature and character of God demands that He rescue those whom He loves. When confronted with a crisis, like David, you can put your life in His hands.

Lord, when all is lost I thank You that You reach out to
me with Your mighty hand of rescue. Your welcoming
hand is a lifeline in any storm.

TRIALS HAVE A PURPOSE

*Then Joseph said to his brothers, "Please come closer
to me." And they came closer. And he said, "I am your
brother Joseph, whom you sold into Egypt. And now do
not be grieved or angry with yourselves, because you sold
me here, for God sent me before you to preserve life."*

GENESIS 45:4–5

How many of us could forgive as Joseph did? His jealous siblings had kidnapped him, thrown him into a pit, and then allowed him to be sold into slavery. Yet Joseph trusted that from God's perspective, not his own, his trials had a purpose.

Joseph walked through his humiliating ordeal with his eyes focused on the Lord. He continued not only to love his brothers but to find forgiveness in his heart for them. Studying his life has enabled me to look at my own situation differently: God can accomplish miracles in the midst of trials.

Is there a hurt so deep inside that you have never shared it with another human being? Perhaps someone in your own family has rejected or betrayed you. Remember the pain suffered by Joseph; remember the anguish of Jesus Christ, who was betrayed by one as close as a brother, Judas Iscariot. God knows your pain, and He is strong enough to remove any burden.

*Lord, sometimes I want to enjoy my agony a while
longer. Show me the brilliance of Your forgiveness that
I might trust You in the trial and not miss the outcome
You've planned.*

A Life Turned Around

The man said, "Who made you ruler and judge over us? Are you thinking of killing me as you killed the Egyptian?" Then Moses was afraid and thought, "What I did must have become known."
Exodus 2:14 NIV

Moses had killed an Egyptian. And the action he thought he'd taken in secret had been observed. Why had he killed the man? Because Moses as a Jew, miraculously delivered by God from certain death, could not stand by and watch an Egyptian beating a fellow Hebrew. Was it right? No. God Himself administers true justice, in His own time, to those who deserve punishment.

Later, on Mount Horeb, Moses encountered the living God when he saw a burning bush. "'Moses! Moses!'" called God's voice from the fiery bush. "'I am the God of your father, the God of Abraham, the God of Isaac and the God of Jacob'" (Exodus 3:6 NIV).

Then God revealed His plan to Moses, a plan to bring the Israelites out of Egypt. So when Moses asks God, "'Who am I that I should go to Pharaoh and bring the Israelites out of Egypt?'", it comes from the heart of one who has murdered and knows His guilt before God. But instead of rebuke Moses hears, "'I will be with you. . .I am who I am'" (Exodus 3:11–12, 14 NIV). This is the same "I Am" who calls you to serve Him today.

Lord, Moses felt unworthy to serve You because of his great sin. Forgive me of my sins and focus my life on You.

Who is Christ to You?

"But what about you?" he asked. "Who do you say I am?" Simon Peter answered, "You are the Messiah, the Son of the living God."
MATTHEW 16:15–16 NIV

Jesus repeatedly asked this question to those who followed after Him. He knew that in a short while He would be gone from the face of the earth and all these fledgling Christians would have to bolster their faith were His words and actions. Jesus wanted to be sure they understood.

Jesus knew that once He was gone His followers would be scattered and most would die for their faith in Him. Therefore, it was crucial that they understand exactly who Christ was.

Six days after this conversation with Peter a miraculous event occurred. Jesus took Peter, James, and John up a high mountain. And there He was transfigured before them. "His face shone like the sun, and His garments became as white as light" (Matthew 17:2). Moses and Elijah appeared with Jesus and spoke with Him.

A bright cloud overshadowed them and a voice from heaven said, "'This is My beloved Son, with whom I am well-pleased; listen to Him!'" (Matthew 17:5). Just the awesome sound of God's voice caused the disciples to fall on their faces in fear.

Jesus Christ: Son of God, Son of Man, Redeemer, displayed His glory to these disciples. Do you know Him as Savior?

Lord, if I have allowed the world's viewpoint to diminish who You are, let me now see the truth. Let me declare as Peter did, "You are the Christ, the Son of God."

Forsaken by God?

My God, my God, why have You forsaken me?
Far from my deliverance are the words of my groaning.
PSALM 22:1

Have you ever cried out to God with such despairing utterances as these? I have. Amid the deep black void of a moonless night, my loneliness threatened to pull me into a swirling, spiraling eddy of emptiness. The sound of my own raspy voice screamed out from my inmost being: "God, if You really exist, show me how to find You! I don't know where You are!" Church hadn't met my needs. People who promised love only provided pain. While my clenched fists beat against my bedroom wall, twelve years' worth of tears, a maelstrom of anger, hurt, and frustration, flowed freely.

He showed me the cross. The year was 1973. I left my knapsack of grief on the bloodstained ground beneath His wooden cross. And I never looked back. He has met my every need in surprising, miraculous, and incredible ways.

Jesus, separated from the Father because of our sin, reached the ear of God with His own desperation. He experienced for us this ultimate terror. . .that we would never be forsaken or walk alone the road that leads to Calvary.

Where are you today? On the road, walking toward Him? Sitting down, too bewildered to even formulate questions? Or are you kneeling, as I did, right at His bleeding feet?

Lord, no matter what hazards are down the road, You've got a signpost ready to hang on whatever misleading marker is already in the ground. And the Son is shining ahead!

ℱit for ℐervice

*Then Moses said to the Lord, "Please, Lord, I have
never been eloquent, neither recently nor in time past,
nor since You have spoken to Your servant; for I am slow
of speech and slow of tongue."*
EXODUS 4:10

Poor Moses, he still hasn't grasped the point. God
didn't appoint him spokesperson for the Israelites
to watch him fail. So what was the problem? Moses
heard God's voice clearly calling him to this position.
Why was he balking at the task?

But remember that Moses was nothing but
a murderer with the best of intentions when God
first met him at that burning bush. Perhaps he took
a momentary look back at his life before the Lord got
hold of him. The previous Pharaoh had wanted to kill
him. That could definitely have caused him to quake
in his sandals.

The passage continues: "Then the anger of the
Lord burned against Moses, and He said, 'Is there not
your brother Aaron the Levite?. . .he shall speak for
you to the people. . .'" Now if this were God's plan all
along, why was He angry with Moses? Because the
Lord wanted Moses to understand that He could and
would meet all of his needs. Moses needed to understand that God's power is limitless. Instead, Moses
settled for allowing Aaron to speak for him.

Do you give the Lord part of your problem and
then halfway through start solving it yourself?

*Lord, I am inadequate to understand Your perfection.
Please help me see that Your help is like owning a store
that has everything I need, in utterly limitless supply.*

Pharaoh Admits His Sin

Then Pharaoh sent for Moses and Aaron, and said to them, "I have sinned this time; the Lord is the righteous one, and I and my people are the wicked ones."
EXODUS 9:27

One would think that with an admission like this, especially from an unbelieving ruler, the man had finally seen the light. Pharaoh sounds ready to commit his heart and soul to the almighty God. Wrong! Although the Egyptians had already suffered through seven plagues, brought on by Pharaoh's stubborn refusal to allow the Israelites to leave, Pharaoh still wasn't really convinced of God's power.

Even Moses wasn't so easily fooled: "As soon as I go out of the city, I will spread out my hands to the Lord; the thunder will cease, and there will be hail no longer, that you may know that the earth is the Lord's. But as for you and your servants, I know that you do not yet fear the Lord God."

However, because Pharaoh's heart had not yielded to God's authority, as soon as the storm passed he became predictably relentless, again refusing to allow the Israelites to go. Three more plagues would come upon the people because their leader refused to honor the true God.

Pharaoh would pay a terrible price for his sins. In the end his stubbornness would cause the loss of his own precious son. This would be the final curse in Egypt, the death of every firstborn son.

Lord, it's so easy to see Pharaoh's obstinate streak. Give me strength to admit when I'm wrong. Give me strength to come to You in repentance.

RENEWAL OF ALL THINGS

*Then Peter answered and said to Him,
"Behold, we have left everything and followed You;
what then will there be for us?" And Jesus said to them,
"Truly I say to you, that you who have followed Me,
in the regeneration when the Son of Man will sit on His
glorious throne, you also shall sit upon twelve thrones,
judging the twelve tribes of Israel."*
MATTHEW 19:27–28

Peter, always so practical. Here's what he's really saying: "Lord, when we get to the end will it have been worth it to follow You?" And Jesus reassures him with a gigantic yes!

How it must have broken Jesus' heart to know His treasured follower would be martyred one day. Perhaps Peter had an inkling about this too. We see he wanted desperately to know whether life really went on eternally. The Lord went a step further and related that Peter would not only be with Christ, the Son of Man, eternally, but he would have work to do once he arrived in heaven.

None of us will just occupy space in heaven. Our God is always productive. And this job to which Jesus refers, that of judging the twelve tribes of Israel, will be given to the disciples.

Have you ever speculated as to what you might do in heaven? Well, don't worry, it's not going to be anything like what you've done on earth. Your "boss," after all, will be perfect. And the tasks you perform will be custom-tailored to you. "Job satisfaction" will finally fit into our vernacular.

Lord, I can't even imagine what You have in store for me in heaven. Please keep me faithful to complete the duties You've called me to on earth.

27

The Passover Lamb

"Slay the Passover lamb. You shall take a bunch of hyssop and dip it in the blood which is in the basin, and apply some of the blood that is in the basin to the lintel and the two doorposts; and none of you shall go outside the door of his house until morning. For the Lord will pass through to smite the Egyptians; and when He sees the blood on the lintel and on the two doorposts, the Lord will pass over the door and will not allow the destroyer to come to your houses to smite you."

Exodus 12:21–23

This Scripture passage paints a comprehensive picture of the Passover.

Each year this symbolic Passover meal is re-created. The man of the house reads Exodus 12:14. Then his wife puts on her head covering and lights two candles. Using circular motions with her hands above the candles, she then closes her eyes and says a specific prayer.

Four cups of wine or grape juice represent sanctification, the cup of plagues (visited on Egypt), the cup of redemption by Messiah, and the cup of praise to God as the King of the Universe.

Other symbols include parsley, which represents produce, likened to Israel as a seed and growing to maturity; a hidden matzoh bread, denoting Christ in the tomb; the shank bone of the Passover lamb; bitter herbs, commemorating their slavery; and karoset, an apple mixture akin to the mortar of the bricks they made in Egypt as slaves.

We can celebrate the Passover with joy and thanksgiving, knowing for certain that the long-awaited Messiah has come, and will come again!

❧

Lord Jesus Christ, I thank You for being my promised Messiah and Passover Lamb. I thank You for Your sacrifice so that my sins could be forgiven.

An Invitation to Dine

*"The kingdom of heaven may be compared to a king,
who gave a wedding feast for his son. And he sent out his
slaves to call those who had been invited to the wedding
feast, and they were unwilling to come."*
Matthew 22:2–3

Have you ever given a dinner party only to have your guests cancel at the last minute? Perhaps they didn't even offer a decent excuse. You're seething inside. You've worked all day long to prepare your home for these "ungrateful people," who will surely never be invited again.

When God sent His Son to earth, He invited all men and women to a wedding feast. Those who accept the invitation become part of the Church. And the Church is the bride of Christ. But there are many who have offered feeble excuses for their lack of faith.

The Son is the Bridegroom for whom the wedding feast is prepared. God Himself has laid the groundwork in the hearts that will respond to His Son, Jesus Christ.

There will be an appointed hour in the future when the guests will come to the banquet. And Christ will call them forth to be His Church when all is made ready, after His Resurrection and Ascension and the coming of the Holy Spirit at Pentecost.

Also, those in attendance receive "wedding clothes." Jesus Christ now clothes them in His righteousness. Those not wearing these garments are cast out because they refused Christ's invitation, and in so doing, have rejected His salvation.

Lord, You've invited me to dine with You. Let me graciously accept my "wedding clothes."

ℛEMEMBER THE 𝒮ABBATH

"Remember the Sabbath day, to keep it holy.
Six days you shall labor and do all your work,
but the seventh day is a Sabbath of the LORD your God;
in it you shall not do any work. . . For in six days the
Lord made the heavens and the earth, the sea and all
that is in them, and rested on the seventh day."
EXODUS 20:8–11

During the 1950s in Missouri, where I grew up, blue laws virtually shut down the city on Sundays. You could see whole families, dressed in their Sunday best, walking toward the nearest big intersection, where you'd find a different denomination on each corner. The rest of the day might be spent enjoying picnics, bike rides, or "visiting Grandma." I loved those relaxing times with the extended family.

Merchants finally managed to get these laws overturned and the stores opened on Sunday. Sales were timed to begin early on the Sabbath, enticing people to make a choice between church and shopping. On a Sunday morning compare the number of parked cars in the mall with those in the church lots. This worldly strategy has certainly been effective.

In the very beginning of our marriage my husband and I made a decision to honor God on Sunday. He has blessed our family over and over for this faithful commitment, providing not only the weekly spiritual guidance we desperately need, but also giving our bodies and souls the rest they require.

Lord, please help me to remember that Your commandments are always for my good.

Mourning Turned into Dancing

You have turned for me my mourning into dancing.
PSALM 30:11

If you've never read *The Hiding Place* by Corrie ten Boom, it might be difficult to understand how God could turn mourning into dancing. For hiding many Jewish people in their home during World War II, Corrie and her family were imprisoned in a Nazi death camp. Corrie alone survived that ordeal and went on to travel the world, sharing one message: Jesus can turn loss into glory.

Years ago I was drawn to watch Corrie ten Boom one day on television. She spoke about a meeting, long after the war, with the S.S. soldier who had stood guard in the showers at her concentration camp. When I heard her speak about extending her hand in a gesture of forgiveness, her words pierced through my soul like a dagger. How could she offer the hand of friendship to him? Lacking her own strength, Corrie prayed to God for Him to give His forgiveness to this man. And when Corrie's hand touched the former soldier's, she likened it to love's lightning going through her arm, to the man, and then back again.

At the time, there were many people whom I felt incapable of pardoning. God's name topped the list. Corrie's words lingered in my mind and heart, making me miserable. But I finally surrendered my life to Christ. And God's power of forgiveness has turned my own mourning into dancing.

Lord, Your "merry saint," Corrie, knew joy was a condition of a heart filled with forgiveness. Help me see this too!

𝒫ETER'S 𝒟ENIAL

Then Jesus said to them, "You will all fall away because
of Me this night, for it is written, 'I will strike down the
shepherd, and the sheep of the flock shall be scattered.'
But after I have been raised, I will go ahead of you to
Galilee." But Peter said to Him, "Even though all may
fall away because of You, I will never fall away."
MATTHEW 26:31–33

Peter was convinced that his faith in Christ was so strong nothing could cause it to crumble. Yet only a few hours later he cowered when a young servant girl accused him of being one of Jesus' followers. And then he openly denied his Lord.

How boldly he had declared, "'Even if I have to die with You, I will not deny You'" (Matthew 26:35). And all the rest of the disciples verbally agreed with Peter. A little while later they accompanied Jesus into the Garden of Gethsemane, where He requested that they pray with Him. Instead, they fell asleep.

Later that night, Peter would know without any doubt that Jesus had tried to warn him. Then he would look into those intense eyes and understand that because Christ went to Calvary even this sin of denial could be forgiven.

There have been times when you have disappointed Jesus. Have you asked for forgiveness? Have you realized that upon asking the burden of sin will be lifted forever?

Lord, I have, at one time or another, acted as if I could
live any way I wanted. Yet it cost Christ everything to
purchase my redemption. Let me willingly come and
pray to You.

BEFORE HE SET THE HEAVENS IN PLACE

"The Lord possessed me at the beginning of His way,
Before His works of old. From everlasting I was estab-
lished, From the beginning, from the earliest times of the
earth. When there were no depths I was brought forth,
When there were no springs abounding with water. . .
When He marked out the foundations of the earth;
Then I was beside Him, as a master workman."
PROVERBS 8:22–24, 29–30

What existed before anything else? God. And now woman and man come along, filling in a narrow blip of time, and state that all of creation "just simply evolved." Get a clue! God designed, planned, and implemented all that we do see and everything we can't comprehend.

We've already discussed how Solomon asked God for wisdom that he might rule more fairly. In answer, the Lord imparted to him a veritable wealth of knowledge about this extraordinary creation.

In questioning Job, God provides more information about the creation. "'Have you ever in your life commanded the morning, and caused the dawn to know its place, that it might take hold of the ends of the earth, and the wicked be shaken out of it?'" (Job 38:12–13) Or, "'Where were you when I laid the foundation of the earth?'" (Job 38:4).

Somehow we have turned around history. Humans are not in charge. God is. And He's still commanding the dawn to happen and the earth to keep spinning and the stars to remain in the sky. Aren't you glad?

Lord, keep me from taking Your magnificence for granted.
Let my heart overflow with gratitude for all You are.

OFFERINGS FOR THE TENT OF MEETING

Then the whole Israelite community withdrew from
Moses' presence, and everyone who was willing and
whose heart moved them came and brought an offering
to the Lord for the work on the tent of meeting,
for all its service, and for the sacred garments.
EXODUS 35:20–21 NIV

When was the last time your whole community agreed on anything? Imagine everyone's talents, skills, and resources united for a common purpose!

The hearts of God's people were stirred to erect the Tent of Meeting, following the Lord's command. Leaving all selfish desires behind, they pooled their brooches, earrings, signet rings, bracelets, and other offerings of gold for the Lord. From these articles gemstones were extracted to make the ephod and the breastpiece.

Women spun goats' hair cloth and fine linen. Silver, bronze, and acacia wood were also contributed, along with spices and oil for the fragrance, light, and anointing within the traveling temple. Then the Lord raised up those who would skillfully engrave, design, or embroider materials. In the hands of the Master Builder, our human talents soar!

As those in Moses' day brought all they possessed, we can surrender our own time and talents. A dear "saint" at my own church writes notes of encouragement to all who request prayer. How blessed we are to receive her "wisdom from the Lord" when we're depleted by life's challenges.

How is God using you in His church?

Lord, You've created within me something to be used to further Your Kingdom. Please enable me to open my hands willingly in service.

TRUE LOVE MEANS SACRIFICE

And they spat on Him, and took the reed and began to beat Him on the head. After they had mocked Him, they took the scarlet robe off Him and put His own garments back on Him, and led Him away to crucify Him.
MATTHEW 27:30–31

Years ago the popular movie *Love Story* coined the unforgettable phrase, "Love means never having to say you're sorry." What a fallacy, and more is the pity for those who bought into this lie!

For love demands that we always say we're sorry. How else can relationships be restored? Those two words, "I'm sorry," have the power to keep families and churches together. I once knew a pastor whose refusal to recognize his humanity caused almost half of the church family to seek membership elsewhere. In his eyes he had done nothing wrong, but what harm would have been done to admit the possibility of poor judgment?

To admit fallibility is to make a sacrifice. To have done nothing wrong and to offer the ultimate sacrifice is an act only possible by God's Son. Jesus' offering of His body at Calvary gave eternal life to all who believe in Him.

Is there someone from whom you are estranged who is waiting to hear those two little words? Say you're sorry.

Lord, You sacrificed all You had to provide my eternal salvation. Help me today to express true sorrow for my sins.

Offerings to the Lord

*"Speak to the sons of Israel and say to them,
'When any man of you brings an offering to the Lord,
you shall bring your offerings of animals from
the herd or the flock.' "*
LEVITICUS 1:2

God communicated His Word and His desire for proper worship through His chosen leaders. These spokesmen then communicated His message to His chosen people. Before the coming of the Holy Spirit, at Pentecost, this chain of command was vital so that God's flock was not misled.

God required proper and orderly worship. Only an unblemished male animal could be used as the burnt offering. Down through the ages men and women were to make a connection between this sacrifice and the one Christ would willingly make on Calvary's cross.

The priests carried out God's specific requirements for slaughtering the animal, sprinkling its blood against the altar and cutting and arranging these pieces in a certain order. Finally, the sacrifice was burned upon the wood. And when these instructions were carried out they made a "pleasing aroma" to the Lord.

There have not been any animal sacrifices since the temple in Jerusalem was destroyed in AD 70. Since Christ made His atoning sacrifice on the cross, our sins are forgiven based on His shed blood.

Lord, how grateful I am for Jesus, Your unblemished Lamb. Might I willingly become a living sacrifice through service to You as I take the Gospel to this needy world.

A Woman of Folly

The woman of folly is boisterous, She is naive, and knows nothing. She sits at the doorway of her house, On a seat by the high places of the city, Calling to those who pass by, who are making their paths straight: "Whoever is naive, let him turn in here," And to him who lacks understanding she says, "Stolen water is sweet; And bread eaten in secret is pleasant." But he does not know. . .the depths of Sheol.

PROVERBS 9:13–18

This woman is beyond sanguine. She is the party, not just the life of it! But how did she end up this way, sitting at the doorway of her house and calling out to those who pass by?

Perhaps life has just sort of happened to her, and she lost the battle before she even knew what the war was about. When she was young, all the road signs appeared to be filled with possibilities. But now that she's getting older the options are fewer. She's sitting on a suitcase in an abandoned train station, waiting for the whistle to blow again.

This woman is not only content to wreak havoc on her own life, but she entices those who wanted to go the right way to join her on this road to nowhere. The passage describes her "naive," because surely if she'd known better she'd have chosen more wisely.

Have you ever felt like this woman? Did you start out with endless options and then begin purchasing tickets to oblivion? With Christ it's not too late to cash in that pass to nowhere. With Christ your life will have direction.

Lord, please provide me with a true picture of myself. Guide me to the place You envision for me.

To Touch Jesus' Cloak

*A woman who had a hemorrhage for twelve years,
and had endured much at the hands of many physicians,
and had spent all that she had and was not helped at
all, but rather had grown worse, after hearing about
Jesus, she came up in the crowd behind Him and
touched His cloak. For she thought, "If I just touch
His garments, I will get well."*
MARK 5:25–28

This woman is frantic. Each time she's received the report of a gifted healer, she's traversed far and wide to find a cure. The wonder is that this dear woman could survive for twelve long years. For that phrase, "endured much," means she "suffered something or experienced evil." She'd become a challenge to physicians of that day.

In one last-ditch effort she reaches out to touch the garment of Jesus as He passes by. She doesn't bother to call out to Him or even ask for help. Somehow she knows that His very holiness can heal her physically.

"Immediately Jesus, perceiving in Himself that the power proceeding from Him had gone forth, turned around in the crowd and said, 'Who touched My garments?'" (Mark 5:30). The disciples think He's "losing it" for sure.

"But the woman fearing and trembling, aware of what had happened to her, came and fell down before Him and told Him the whole truth" (Mark 5:33). She's been miraculously healed and now she demonstrates her faith by worshiping at Jesus' feet. Does your faith shine through even in small gestures?

Lord, You heal me when I come to You, by renewing my spirit and deepening my faith. I worship Your majesty and power.

The Lord's Diet Plan

"Speak to the sons of Israel, saying, 'These are the creatures which you may eat from all the animals that are on the earth. Whatever divides a hoof, thus making split hoofs, and chews the cud, among the animals, that you may eat.'"

LEVITICUS 11:2

Ever gone on a diet? As soon as you start one, the compulsion to eat things you never desired before becomes an overpowering beast! We know that the right foods are good for us, but we can't block out the joyfully intoxicating flavors of the ones that are off-limits.

Since Moses was chosen by God to deliver these dietary restrictions to the Israelites, we can well imagine the rousing response he received. Leviticus 11 goes on to list creatures that fall into the categories of "clean" and "unclean."

The one meat you probably already know about is pork. God didn't even want the Israelites to touch it. He told Moses that although it has "'a divided hoof, does not chew the cud; it is unclean for you'" (Leviticus 11:7 NIV).

Unlike the cow, the pig doesn't take time to ruminate. So what in the world does this have to do with anything?

In those days prior to refrigeration and pasteurization, if the Israelites hadn't obeyed God's dietary laws most if not all of them would have died from bacterial infections, food poisoning, and so on. God was preserving a nation from which the Messiah would be born.

Lord, Your call to obedience may not always make sense, but help me remember that You have a reason.

U-HAULS *D*ON'T *F*OLLOW *H*EARSES

Lord, make me to know my end, And what is the extent
of my days, Let me know how transient I am.
Behold, You have made my days as handbreadths,
And my lifetime as nothing in Your sight,
Surely every man at his best is a mere breath.

PSALM 39:4–5

From the rich and famous to the poor and hopeless, inestimable numbers of women and men consult astrologers before making major decisions. As Christians we know that no human possesses the ability to access knowledge of future events. The attribute of omniscience, being all-knowing, belongs to God alone.

Our human nature propels us to locate a "celestial video" of our own life, including our ultimate demise. So why didn't God just relate this information?

God wants us to trust Him for our future. To know our lifespan would affect us every day of our life. So, God has guarded this secret as a great favor to us.

In a church we used to attend, the pastor was famous for his story about the man who wanted to have a "U-haul following the hearse" to his funeral. The point of his sermon, of course, was that none of us will take the fruits of our labor with us to our eternal destination. Instead we should concern ourselves with where that final stop will be.

To worry about the future is to be uncertain of your eternity.

❦

Lord, it's so easy to get caught up in the glitter of gold.
Give me a daily glimpse of heaven, my real home.

The Wise of Heart

The wise of heart will receive commands,
But a babbling fool will be ruined.
He who walks in integrity walks securely, But he
who perverts his ways will be found out.
PROVERBS 10:8–9

For years James Dobson, president of Focus on the Family, has warned parents about the pitfalls ahead for their strong-willed children. Personally, we raised our three kids with one hand on the radio and the other on the Bible. Dr. Dobson's radio ministry has given us hope and kept us sane.

My repeated prayer for all our children was this: "Lord, protect them and surround them with Your angels. And if they're disobedient, let them be found out."

Years into their teens, our kids were convinced that I had spies stationed all over the city. No matter what they did, I knew about it within hours. And I can assure you, it was a direct result of this prayer. God provided such excellent guidance for us, He entrusted eight other children into our care who were not our own. These young people were just kids who needed special care along the way. We tended to their physical needs as well as their spiritual ones. We stressed honesty and obedience and showered them with unconditional love. And each of them grew to a more secure emotional place.

Is there a young person in your life who needs your prayers today?

Lord, help us to stress honesty, obedience, and the truth of Your Word and shower our kids with unconditional love so that our children can grow to maturity in a secure emotional place.

ʃESUS ᗪRIVES ᗷUT A ᗪEMON

Jesus left that place and went to the vicinity of Tyre.
He entered a house and did not want anyone to know it;
yet he could not keep his presence secret. In fact, as soon as
she heard about him, a woman whose little daughter was
possessed by an impure spirit came and fell at his feet.
MARK 7:24–25 NIV

Shocking headlines assault us almost daily, relating the horrors children have inflicted upon other children. We ask, "What in the world is going on?" Yet even during the time of Christ, diabolic forces knew no age barriers.

A Gentile woman of Syrophoenician heritage sought out Jesus. A desperate woman, she recognized that her little daughter was demon possessed.

She not only displayed faith in His ability to heal, but she believed that she had the right to ask Him for assistance. Further into the passage note the veiled dialogue between Christ and the woman, which goes something like this. First, she tells Him of her daughter's predicament. He says, "'Let the children be satisfied first, for it is not good to take the children's bread and throw it to the dogs'" (Mark 7:27). Then she answers Him, "'Yes, Lord, but even the dogs under the table feed on the children's crumbs'" (Mark 7:28).

Jesus came to bring the Good News to the Jews first. But this woman, a Gentile, says she needs Jesus' touch too. And He responds to her faith. Ask Jesus to touch your life this day.

Lord, You are Messiah to all, Jews and Gentiles, and I know You will never turn me away. In this I rejoice!

COMMANDMENTS OR SUGGESTIONS?

*"You shall consecrate yourselves therefore and be holy,
for I am the Lord your God. And you shall keep My
statutes and practice them; I am the Lord who sanctifies
you. . .You are therefore to keep all My statutes and all
My ordinances and do them, so that the land to which
I am bringing you to live will not spew you out."*
LEVITICUS 20:7–8, 22

When God gave the Laws to Moses, writing them with His own hand upon the tablets of stone, He expected them to be observed. From His perspective they were commandments, not "suggestions."

But how could sinful men ever comply consistently with these laws? Therefore, throughout Old Testament history humanity was to look forward in time and trust God for the coming Messiah. And His death would finally cleanse them from their sin. Abraham believed this and passed the "promise" on to his descendants. Isaac then brought this seed of expectation to Jacob. And on and on the word of the Lord progressed.

However, so did man's sin. Because God had endowed each person with a free will. Our hope lies in the fact that Jesus Christ has paid the penalty for all our sin, on Calvary's cross, no matter how heinous it might be. And if we confess our sins to Him, then He is faithful and just to forgive us (1 John 1:9).

*Lord, having a relationship with You is the only way
we can keep Your commands. Help us to relinquish our
wills to You.*

JESUS IS TRANSFIGURED

Jesus took with Him Peter and James and John... And
He was transfigured before them; and His garments
became radiant and exceedingly white, as no launderer
on earth can whiten them. And Elijah appeared to them
along with Moses; and they were talking with Jesus.
MARK 9:2–4

We can't even imagine what glory these disciples beheld. Their human eyes were allowed to view Jesus virtually transformed into a supernatural form.

Moses and Elijah also appeared with Christ. Moses represented the Law and Elijah the prophets, both of which find their fulfillment in Christ. We know from the Scriptures that when Satan wanted to take Moses' body God took him away instead. And no one knows where Moses is buried (Deuteronomy 34:6). Similarly, Elijah was taken up to heaven by a whirlwind and never died (2 Kings 2:1–11). Furthermore, it was prophesied that Elijah would come back before the end of time (Malachi 4:5). In fact, John the Baptist preached in the "spirit and power of Elijah" (Luke 1:16–17).

The Greek word for this phenomenon of transfiguration is *metamorphoo*, from which we derive our word metamorphosis. Christ performs the miracle of metamorphosis in us when we come to believe in Him as Lord and Savior. He transforms us, quickening our spirits, so that we are destined to spend eternity with God in heaven. It's a change on the inside that is displayed on the outside—for the unbelieving world to see.

Lord, transform me today, by Your Almighty power,
into a bold witness of Your Gospel message.

In Memory of the Righteous

The memory of the righteous is blessed,
But the name of the wicked will rot.
PROVERBS 10:7

Not long ago I attended the funeral of the mother of one of my husband's coworkers. Although I'd never met this man or his mother, knowing that his family had come from the Philippines drew me to the service. With their homeland so far away, perhaps there wouldn't be many in attendance.

Warmth, love, and appreciation greeted my husband and me from the moment we set foot in the chapel, which overflowed with guests. Somehow this large family had assembled to provide a magnificent send-off for their precious "Nanay." Amid the battles of World War II, she was widowed at twenty-seven and left with three small children. Yet those difficult days of grief and hardship became her stepping-stones to faith in Christ. Later she remarried and was blessed with five more children.

Her parting admonition to the children who gathered around her deathbed was "be good and love each other." And then her Lord peacefully escorted her to the mansion He'd prepared.

This woman had lost so much. And yet, blessed with true wisdom, she turned to the Lord for solace and found in Him the foundation on which to build her life. To leave a rich legacy of love one must be dearly acquainted with the Author of Love, our Heavenly Father.

Lord, I am blessed by the memory of righteous women.
Help me to live in such a worthy manner, that I might
be remembered as following after You all my days.

JESUS PROPHESIES HIS DEATH

They were amazed, and those who followed were fearful.
And again He took the twelve aside and began to tell
them what was going to happen to Him, saying,
"Behold, we are going up to Jerusalem, and the Son of
Man will be delivered to the chief priests and the scribes;
and they will condemn Him to death, and will deliver
Him to the Gentiles. And they will mock Him and
spit upon Him, and scourge Him, and kill Him,
and three days later He will rise again."

MARK 10:32–34

When our family received the ominous news that my father-in-law was terminally ill, I struggled to prepare myself for the grief. Instead, I ended up making myself physically ill. I soon reached the conclusion that I just needed to enjoy my father-in-law's presence for as long as God kept him here on earth. And when our inevitable time of mourning did descend upon our hearts, the Lord would pour out His magnanimous grace toward us.

Christ's disciples couldn't cope with the thought of His leaving and therefore became fearful. Jesus gently encouraged them with the hope of His resurrection.

And when He had risen from the dead, "He opened their minds to understand the Scriptures, and He said to them, 'Thus it is written, that the Christ should suffer and rise again from the dead the third day; and that repentance for the forgiveness of sins should be proclaimed in His name to all the nations, beginning from Jerusalem. You are witnesses of these things'" (Luke 24:45–48).

Lord, when grief overwhelms us let us remember Your death on Calvary's cross provides our hope of eternal life in heaven.

God Orders a Census

*"Take a census of all the congregation of the sons of
Israel, by their families, by their fathers' households,
according to the number of names, every male,
head by head from twenty years old and upward,
whoever is able to go out to war in Israel, you and Aaron
shall number them by their armies. With you, moreover,
there shall be a man of each tribe, each one head
of his father's household."*

Numbers 1:2–4

Have you ever watched small children begin to play?
Some just observe toys, randomly tossing them about
until they find one that really grabs their attention.
Others begin with an overall plan. Now we can chalk
up this inborn sense of order to personality, parental
patterning, and so on. But I believe all ages participate
in creational emulation, in response to the perfect
established order of God.

The Israelites, who were constantly at odds
with the Gentile nations surrounding them, needed
to know the strength of their army. So God showed
Moses a systematic way to determine this number.

Notice that men were conscripted to serve Israel's
army from the time they were twenty years old until
they were no longer able to serve. In doing so, they
would be preserving their nation clear into the time in
history when Messiah would finally be born.

*Lord, with You everything has a plan. In a world that
is filled with nebulous thinking I can rely on Your
consistency.*

By Whose Authority Did Jesus Act?

The chief priests and the scribes and the elders came to Him, and began saying to Him, "By what authority are You doing these things, or who gave You this authority to do these things?" And Jesus said to them, "I will ask you one question, and you answer Me, and then I will tell you by what authority I do these things. Was the baptism of John from heaven, or from men? Answer Me."

MARK 11:27–30

One of the mental exercises I wrestled with in a basic psychology course in college concerned unanswerable questions. You've probably seen them on employment tests: For example, "What would you say is your least desirable personality trait?" Now who is going to answer this without trying to put a positive spin on it?

This is the kind of squeeze play the Pharisees and Scribes tried constantly to force Jesus into. No matter what Jesus said, He'd be wrong. And yet this tactic always backfired on them.

The Pharisees, the Jewish religious leaders, made sure the Mosaic laws were adhered to. They read the laws day and night, probably looking for ones that had been broken. The scribes were given the task of recording every "jot and tittle" of the Word of God. Both groups not only knew the law but also understood what the Messiah would do when He came.

Jesus Christ cannot be fooled. He knew the hearts of the Pharisees and scribes and He knows your heart too.

Jesus, You spoke plainly about who You are. Help me hear.

Never Take a Drink?

Again the Lord spoke to Moses, saying, "Speak to the sons of Israel, and say to them, 'When a man or woman makes a special vow, the vow of a Nazarite, to dedicate himself to the LORD, he shall abstain from wine and strong drink; he shall drink no vinegar, whether made from wine or strong drink, neither shall he drink any grape juice, nor eat fresh or dried grapes. All the days of his separation he shall not eat anything that is produced by the grape vine, from the seeds even to the skin. All the days of his vow of separation no razor shall pass over his head. He shall be holy until the days are fulfilled for which he separated himself to the Lord, he shall let the locks of hair on his head grow long.'"

NUMBERS 6:1–5

My few experiences drinking liquor as a young woman convinced me it tasted awful and it had an extremely negative effect on my emotions.

When I became a Christian, at age twenty-nine, drinking was the first thing to go out of my life. Along with all the warnings against strong drink that I read in the Bible, there was family history. My father had been an alcoholic.

After making a decision to follow Christ, I recognized the risk of potentially harming the young children my husband and I were raising. Like a Nazarite submitting to his vow, I refused to provide a breeding ground in which this substance might interfere with the plans God desired for my life and future. And the Lord has remained faithful to provide all the inspiration I need.

Whatever is preventing me from seeing only You, Lord, provide the strength I require to set it aside.

David Called Him Lord

And Jesus began to say, as He taught in the temple,
"How is it that the scribes say that the Christ is the son of
David? David himself said in the Holy Spirit, 'The Lord
said to my Lord, "Sit at My right hand, Until I put thine
enemies beneath Your feet.'" David himself calls Him
'Lord'; and so in what sense is He his son?" And the great
crowd enjoyed listening to Him. And in His teaching He
was saying: "Beware of the scribes. . .who devour widows'
houses, and for appearance's sake offer long prayers;
these will receive greater condemnation."
MARK 12:35–38, 40

In this age where all of us are overly conscious of being politically correct, it's difficult to understand how extremely direct Christ was being here. The Pharisees, after all, enjoyed a position in which their motives and actions were seldom questioned.

Christ had just explained to the Pharisees that the reason they couldn't comprehend what would take place in the Resurrection was because they understood neither the Scriptures nor the power of God (Mark 12:24).

All of us are responsible not only to read the Word of God with understanding but also to have discernment concerning the clergy who minister to us. Is their primary goal to make sure their flock is ultimately led to God's glory?

Am I like those in the crowd who simply "enjoyed listen-
ing" to Christ? Help me take time to know You, Lord.

WALKING IN THE LIGHT OF GOD'S GOODNESS

*The fear of the Lord prolongs life, But the years of the
wicked will be shortened. The hope of the rightous is
gladness, But the expectation of the wicked perishes.
The way of the LORD is a stronghold to the upright,
But ruin to the workers of iniquity. The rightous will
never be shaken, but the wicked will not dwell in the land.*

PROVERBS 10:27–30

Instead of being a cause of terror in our hearts, that
phrase, "fear of the Lord" means to reverence and
honor Him as God. For He alone is God, righteous,
and wise enough to intervene and effect positive
changes in our lives. Instilling this truth in our children enables them to know the ways of the Lord.

Knowing that everything that emanates from
God is good enables us to trust Him in every crisis
and walk in His ways. Because in each situation there
are two alternative reactions. On the one hand exists
the opportunity to act honorably, and on the other
freedom to disobey. The choice is entirely ours.

God's very nature is goodness. Therefore, everything that stems from Him reflects His character.
This knowledge should cause hope to flood our lives.
Unshaken by the winds of change, then we can stand
firm in the face of any kind of adversity, like a boat
anchored to its strong moorings.

Obedience always brings inner peace, content-
ment, and happiness, while stepping out from under-
neath God's umbrella of protection only gets us
soaked and saturated with sin.

*Lord, show us how to raise children who reflect the
goodness of Your character!*

Sinners from Birth

Behold I was brought forth in iniquity,
And in sin my mother conceived me.
Psalm 51:5

When Kay Arthur of Precept Ministries had just become a grandmother, she stated in one of her ministry updates, "Well, another little sinner was just born into the world!"

This might seem a strange thing to say about one's precious, be it ever so wrinkled, grandbaby. And yet it's the absolute truth. David knew this thousands of years ago as he was inspired to write this psalm.

You need to get straight in this passage what God's Word is not saying. The union of man and woman, within the bounds of marriage, is absolutely God's design and purpose. These verses are not alluding to the act of love that produces a child. Rather, David is stating that each of us is born with the same sin nature as Adam.

David spoke from the depths of his guilty, broken heart. He had viewed the lovely Bathsheba as she prepared to bathe on her rooftop. Hypnotized by her beauty he "took her to bed." And when she became pregnant, he plotted a murderous solution that would send her husband, Uriah, to the front lines of battle.

Admitting our own sinful state is the first step toward a more sincere Christian walk. And acknowledging the sin in our children makes us more effective Christian parents.

David didn't acknowledge his sin until You sent Nathan the prophet to convict his soul. What will it take for me, Lord?

SIBLING RIVALRY

Then the Lord called Aaron and Miriam. . .He said,
"Hear now My words: If there is a prophet among you,
I the LORD, shall make Myself known to him in a vision.
I shall speak with him in a dream. Not so, with My
servant Moses, He is faithful in all My household;
With him I speak mouth to mouth, Even openly,
And not in dark sayings, and he beholds the form of the
Lord. Why then were you not afraid To speak against
My servant, against Moses?"
NUMBERS 12:5–8

Sibling rivalry has once again reared its ugly head. God speaks face-to-face with Moses, and Aaron and Miriam become jealous. So God comes down in a pillar of cloud to announce to them that this is His show and He writes the script. When the cloud is withdrawn from over the Tent of Meeting, Miriam's skin has become leprous.

Like a good parent, God leaves Miriam to mull over her rebellious and questioning spirit for seven days. And then the Lord graciously heals her, at the request of Moses.

How could she even think of asking God to explain Himself? But don't we all do the same thing when the going gets rough? How about, "If there's a God then why is there so much suffering?" Well, guess what? Men and women are harming one another. God is not responsible for our sinful nature.

The power to make a choice between good and evil is a gift from God. What we do with the gift is up to us.

Lord, although it's human to question things beyond my control, please help me understand that Your actions are always in my best interest.

WHEN FEAR PARALYZES

And a certain young man was following Him, wearing nothing but a linen sheet over his naked body; and they seized him. But he left the linen sheet behind, and escaped naked. And they led Jesus away to the high priest; and all the chief priests and the elders and the scribes gathered together. Peter had followed Him at a distance, right into the courtyard of the high priest; and he was sitting with the officers, and warming himself at the fire. Now the chief priests and the whole Council kept trying to obtain testimony against Jesus to put Him to death; and they were finding none.

MARK 14:51–55

Suddenly you awake at one in the morning to the sound of the doorknob being turned, followed by the sound of creaking boards. Your heart leaps into your throat. What do you do?

When John Mark, the writer of this Gospel, learned that Jesus had been captured by the Roman guards and a trial was pending, he grabbed the sheet off his bed and ran to observe the events himself.

We know John Mark escaped the threatening situation. Yet Jesus Christ remained in the eye of the storm, well aware of the situation yet in perfect sync with the Father. When fear paralyzes, help is only a prayer away.

Lord, I believe in all that You are, both God and Man.

BARABBAS IS RELEASED

*Pilate answered them, saying, "Do you want me to
release for you the King of the Jews?" . . .But the chief
priests stirred up the multitude to ask him to release
Barabbas for them instead. And answering again,
Pilate said to them, "Then what shall I do with Him
whom you call the King of the Jews?"
And they shouted back, "Crucify Him!"*
MARK 15:9, 11–13

During the Feast of the Passover, Pilate had a habit of releasing one prisoner back to the people. The people cried out for the release of a known murderer, Barabbas.

Why did the chief priests incite the people to choose Barabbas? So many had chosen willingly to follow Christ that the "status quo" of the times had been upset.

After all, the chief priests had a nice cushy job making up laws to enforce so that the people were kept in a constant state of guilt. The priests' coffers were kept full from the constant flow of guilt offerings. If Jesus were allowed to gain a foothold in the temple, their positions would surely be in jeopardy.

The priests were but players in the great drama prophesied hundreds of years earlier in the Old Testament. Jesus Christ would be sentenced to death by Pilate, even though Pilate found Him without guilt. Jesus Christ must die for the sins of humankind.

Today we know the truth. And we can share, without fear, without guilt, the kingship of Jesus Christ.

What would I have shouted if I had been part of that crowd? And what affirmation do I give You today, Lord?

JOSEPH OF ARIMATHEA

*Joseph of Arimathea. . .gathered up courage and went in
before Pilate, and asked for the body of Jesus.*
MARK 15:43

Today's Scripture reading, along with parallel passages from the other three Gospels, discloses that Joseph of Arimathea had become "a secret disciple of Christ." Yet now, accompanied by Nicodemus, another member of the ruling Council of religious leaders, Joseph of Arimathea displayed an incredible boldness of character. For Joseph requested Christ's body for burial, then he and Nicodemus lovingly prepared their Lord for his burial.

Christ nurtured the faith of both these men, safely reserving them for His divine purpose within the realm of authority in which He had placed them. They were needed for just such a time, because down through the ages to come the faith of other believers would hinge on the fact that Christ really died and really was resurrected. Fulfilling Scripture, Christ was placed in the borrowed tomb of a rich man (Isaiah 53:9).

Joseph, present during the sessions in which the Council members solidified decisions concerning Christ, never consented to their plan of action. For Joseph was "a good and righteous man" (Luke 23:50–51). Nicodemus also stood his ground despite the growing tide of voices that called for Christ's arrest and crucifixion (John 7:45–53). These men had been born again through their faith in Christ. And knowing the Scriptures concerning the death of their Savior, they prepared for it.

*Lord, the tomb is empty and the grave clothes left behind
signify for all time that You have risen from the dead. And
because You live, we can face whatever tomorrow brings!*

Where Do You Take Refuge?

Be gracious, O God, for man has trampled upon me;
Fighting all day long he oppresses me. My foes have
trampled upon me all day long, For they are many who
fight proudly against me. When I am afraid, I will put
my trust in You. In God, whose word I praise,
In God I have put my trust; I shall not be afraid.
What can mere man do to me?
PSALM 56:1–4

When my father was away during World War II, my mom, sister, and I lived with my grandparents. At the time I was only three years old or so. Frequently, I'd hide under their long, wooden porch, making my world a little smaller, I suppose. Looking out through the latticed covering, somehow I felt safe.

David wrote this psalm when the Philistines had seized him in Gath. These Philistines had been enemies of the Israelites for a long time. At one point they'd even stolen the ark of the covenant. They'd probably never forgiven David for killing their giant, Goliath. I wonder if David reflected during his present predicament, remembering the time in his youth when he'd faced that giant with only five smooth stones and a sling. He had called upon his God to deliver him, and the Lord had prevailed (1 Samuel 17:37–50).

Where do you go for refuge? I run to the arms of my loving Father, just as David did in his own crisis. And He always comes through.

O Lord, You alone are my refuge and strength. Help me to come to You first in a crisis.

John the Baptist is Born

*In the days of Herod, king of Judea, there was a certain
priest named Zacharias, of the division of Abijah;
and he had a wife from the daughters of Aaron, and
her name was Elizabeth. And they were both righteous
in the sight of God, walking blamelessly in all the
commandments and requirements of the Lord.
And they had no child, because Elizabeth was barren,
and they were both advanced in years.*
Luke 1:5–7

What the world would have lost if Zacharias had
become bitter over his circumstances! He and
Elizabeth were now old and their dream of sons and
daughters had become but a vapor.

Zacharias could be found day after day in the
temple, obediently "performing his priestly service
before God" (Luke 1:8).

One day, as he offered incense before the altar,
an angel of the Lord appeared and said, "'Do not be
afraid, Zacharias, for your petition has been heard,
and your wife Elizabeth will bear you a son, and you
will give him the name John'" (Luke 1:13).

Now Zacharias asked, "'How shall I know this
for certain?'" (Luke 1:18). Fulfillment of that promise
still looked impossible to him.

So, poor Zacharias was struck "dumb." Elizabeth
did become pregnant, just as the angel had said. And
during her sixth month, her cousin, Mary, came to tell
her that she too was carrying a child. One day their
sons would meet by the Jordan River. This was God's
perfect plan, the fulfillment of His promises.

Lord, restore my hope in You today.

God's Deterrent to Sin

So Israel joined themselves to Baal of Peor, and the Lord was angry against Israel. And the Lord said to Moses, "Take all the leaders of the people and execute them in broad daylight before the Lord, so that the fierce anger of the Lord may turn away from Israel."

NUMBERS 25:3–4

The Lord had blessed Israel with precious children, remaining true to His promise to Abraham to make the nation of Israel "'as numerous as the stars'" (Genesis 15:5). But when the Israelites began to intermarry with the Moabites they also began to worship their pagan gods. And one of the requirements of this idolatrous form of worship was human sacrifices to the insatiable god Baal. The Israelites thus offered up their children—the gifts of God—to this manmade statue.

God had watched over Israel in war and in peace. He had delivered them safely to a land flowing with milk and honey; He had promised them a Messiah. But if the Israelites continued to kill their children, the line to Christ would be wiped out before He ever arrived on the scene.

God was forced to purge from Israel those who chose to lead others astray.

If you're a parent, you probably devote much time and energy keeping your children from getting involved in things that would harm them. In the same way, God, our loving Parent, must pull in the reins when people drift too far from His truth.

Lord, shine Your beacon of truth on those who are in leadership, that they may never lead others astray.

Anna, the Prophetess

*And there was a prophetess, Anna the daughter of
Phanuel, of the tribe of Asher. . . She never left the
temple, serving night and day with fastings and prayers.
And at that very moment she came up and began giving
thanks to God, and continued to speak of Him to all
those who were looking for the redemption of Jerusalem.*
LUKE 2:36–38

This year, as the National Day of Prayer approached,
one woman in my church did her best to evoke an
enthusiastic response from members of a daytime
Bible study. I watched as many offered her incredu-
lous stares that silently stated, "What planet are you
on? What do you mean, meet for prayer?"

Call a prayer meeting at your own church and
you'll know what I mean. Only a handful of people bother to attend and it's always the same group.
However, if we fail to pray consistently, it is little wonder we are without guidance for our leadership.

Anna had faithfully served in the temple
her entire life. And despite her advanced age, she
remained there even after others had gone home for
the evening. She was a prophetess; she foretold the
truths of God to the people. No wonder He used
her life.

God had promised Anna that she would see
the Messiah before she died. She waited eighty-four
years, biding her time in service to the Lord. And He
kept His Word. Let us strive to follow Anna's prayer-
ful example, and we too will be blessed by God.

*Lord, call my heart to faithfulness and prayer. May I
serve as an example to encourage others.*

God Gave Israel the Land

*Then the Lord spoke to Moses, saying, "Among these the
land shall be divided for an inheritance according to the
number of names. . .each shall be given their inheritance
according to those who were numbered of them.
But the land shall be divided by lot. They shall receive
their inheritance according to the names
of the tribes of their fathers."*
NUMBERS 26:52–55

God picked for Himself a people, the Jews. And He
blessed them with this land as an inheritance. It's not
too late for Israel's enemies to repent. Yet with each
new wave of terrorism and attack against Israel, we
know that nothing short of divine intervention will
free the Jews from annihilation.

One day Christ Himself will return to claim the
Holy Land for His people. "'But immediately after
the tribulation of those days The sun will be darkened, and the moon will not give its light, and the
stars will fall from the sky, and the powers of the
heavens will be shaken, and then the sign of the Son of
Man will appear in the sky, and then all the tribes
of the earth will mourn, and they will see the Son
of Man coming on the clouds of the sky with power
and great glory'" (Matthew 24:29–30).

Christ is coming back as the ultimate Judge and
Rescuer of Israel. The time is now to be sure of our
commitment to Jesus Christ and that of our loved ones.

*Lord, I pray that men and women repent while there
is yet time. I look forward to the establishment of Your
perfect kingdom.*

ONE CALLING IN THE DESERT

The word of God came to John, the son of Zacharias, in the wilderness. And he came into all the district around the Jordan, preaching a baptism of repentance for forgiveness of sins; as it is written in the book of the words of Isaiah the prophet, "The voice of one crying in the wilderness, 'Make ready the way of the Lord, Make his paths straight.'"

LUKE 3:2–4

The Word of God is absolutely specific about the timing, the message, and the messenger, John the Baptist, who paved the way for the Lord Jesus Christ.

As John came into the district around the Jordan River, the religious leaders appeared on the scene to check him out. They used their influence to attempt to dissuade the people from the truth about the Messiah. John called them a "'brood of vipers'" (Luke 3:7). And then he added, "'Therefore bring forth fruits in keeping with repentance, and do not begin to say to yourselves, "We have Abraham for our father," for I say to you that from these stones God is able to raise up children to Abraham'" (Luke 3:8).

Counting on their heritage as a means of automatic salvation, the religious leaders called themselves Abraham's children. Yet to be Abraham's children required that they display faith.

John's exhortations were aimed at the "wilderness of men's souls." How many churchgoers do you know who claim the faith yet exist in a wasteland of sin?

Lord, You sent John to proclaim Your beloved Son. Help me to proclaim Your Word and love to anyone, anywhere.

A Refuge from our Despair

Hear my cry, O God; Give heed to my prayer. From the end of the earth I call to You, when my heart is faint; Lead me to the rock that is higher than I. For You have been a refuge for me, A tower of strength against the enemy. Let me dwell in Your tent forever; Let me take refuge in the shelter of Your wings.

Psalm 61:1–4

King David, writer of this psalm, composed it as a song, acknowledging God as his rock. He clung with tenacity to the fact that no matter how desperate his situation appeared, God was as immovable as a huge rock or boulder. Although David's trials may differ from yours, you too can use strong coping mechanisms.

First, David acknowledged God remained all powerful, despite life circumstances. And second, David looked back at God's past rescues. "O my God, my soul is in despair within me; Therefore I remember You from the land of the Jordan, And the peaks of Hermon, from Mount Mizar. Deep calls to deep at the sound of Your waterfalls; All Your breakers and Your waves have rolled over me. The Lord will command His lovingkindness in the daytime; And His song will be with me in the night, A prayer to the God of my life" (Psalm 42:6–8).

Lord, I search for a way through the torrents of despair. How precious is the knowledge that You hear and care.

WHY MARY AND JOSEPH MARRIED

"Every daughter who comes into possession of an inheritance of the tribe of the sons of Israel, shall be wife to one of the family of the tribe of her father, so that the sons of Israel each may possess the inheritance of his fathers. Thus no inheritance shall be transferred from one tribe to another tribe, for the tribes of the sons of Israel shall each hold to his own inheritance."

NUMBERS 36:8–9

From the time my children were still in grade school, I prayed for the person whom each of them would choose as a life partner in marriage. We spoke often, during those formative years, concerning the foundational qualities needed to forge a lasting relationship. Now that two of our children are married, I can see how God's hand faithfully guided them.

The Gospels of Matthew and Luke present Christ's genealogy. Although Joseph was not Christ's father, he belonged to the tribe of Judah, just as Mary did. Both came from a godly line.

Mary had led a life of purity, revering God's Word and looking forward to the Savior whom God had promised. When God sent an angel to announce His plan, Mary responded in obedience.

Mary and Joseph married because they loved each other but more importantly, both of them loved God and desired to be a part of His purpose for man. And within this environment of submission, Israel's inheritance, the Savior, remained secure.

Lord, we know that Joseph loved Mary and both were chosen by You. Yet they also obeyed you in their choice of a life partner.

Jesus is Tempted by Satan

And the devil said to Him, "If You are the Son of God,
tell this stone to become bread." And Jesus answered him,
"It is written 'Man shall not live on bread alone.'"
LUKE 4:3–4

Have you ever found yourself so tempted to sin that you ached all the way to your soul? Christ understands that pull toward evil.

Satan wasn't just present in the wilderness to "bug" the Lord Jesus Christ. This was a full-on, frontal attack. And the stakes were high. For if Christ succumbed to Satan's snare, He would be ineligible to make that perfect sacrifice on the cross as the Lamb of God without blemish.

In this first temptation, Satan intimated that there must be something wrong with the Father's love for the Son since He allowed Him to go hungry. Satan's fiery darts of doubt were aimed directly at the Triune God.

With the second temptation, Satan led Christ upward for a better view of "all the kingdoms of the world." Satan attempted to get Christ to bypass the cross and seize the power.

The third temptation involved a literal leap of faith. For Satan declared that Jesus prove Himself as the Son of God and stand on the pinnacle of the temple and throw Himself down. This time the evil one meant to question the Father's faithfulness toward the Son. After all, the Scriptures did say that God would give His angels charge concerning Him.

Lord, I thank You for Your Son's perfect victory over Satan.

MATTHEW, THE TAX COLLECTOR

*And after that He went out, and noticed a tax-gatherer
named Levi, sitting in the tax office, and He said to him,
"Follow Me." And he left everything behind, and rose
and began to follow Him. And Levi gave a big
reception for Him in his house; and there was a
great crowd of tax-gatherers and other people
who were reclining at the table with them.*
LUKE 5:27–29

Oh no, not the dreaded tax man! My husband works
in the tax assessor's office for our county. If we attend
a party and people inquire as to what he does for a
living, he skirts the issue. He gets the same reaction
Matthew did.

Yet Levi responded to Christ's invitation to follow
Him. Christ changed his name from Levi to Matthew,
which means "gift of God." Whatever flaws Matthew
possessed prior to this time no longer mattered.

Because of his record-keeping skills and attention
to detail, Matthew made an excellent and meticulous
gospel writer. He'd been regenerated by Christ and
the Lord could use his talents to further the kingdom.

Christ's presence at the reception provided an
opportunity for Him to share the Gospel message.
We too can seek out those whom society shuns and
offer the compassion of Christ.

*Lord, after all these years, attitudes remain the same
about tax collectors. Please help me to see them as You
saw Matthew, as people who know You or are in need
of their Savior.*

MOSES APPOINTS JUDGES

" 'The Lord your God has multiplied you, and behold,
you are this day as the stars of heaven for multitude.
May the Lord, the God of your fathers, increase you
a thousand-fold more than you are, and bless you,
just as He has promised you! Choose wise and discerning
and experienced men from your tribes, and
I will appoint them as your heads.' "

DEUTERONOMY 1:10–13

The Israelites were two million strong when they left Egypt, and now in "the fortieth year, on the first day of the eleventh month" (Deuteronomy. 1:3), Moses proclaimed to them what the Lord had commanded.

The people had been in this same place forty years earlier. But, the Israelites disobeyed God by refusing to fight for the land, and trust God for the victory.

Therefore, God announced that this entire generation of rebellious people, with two exceptions, Caleb and Joshua, would not see the promised land. Even Moses, who had displayed a lack of faith, would not set foot there. God demands trust from His people and His spiritual leaders.

Now that their wandering days were over, Moses charged these twelve tribal officials to judge fairly the disputes among the people. They were about to take possession of the land God had promised them.

Do you trust God for everything?

Dear Heavenly Father, let my trust in You never waver.
Give me wisdom and courage for this day.

Before Choosing the Twelve

He spent the whole night in prayer to God. And when
day came, He called His disciples to Him; and chose
twelve of them, whom He also named as apostles: Simon,
whom He also named Peter, and Andrew his brother;
and James and John; Philip and Bartholomew; Matthew
and Thomas; James the son of Alphaeus, and Simon
who was called the Zealot; Judas the son of James,
and Judas Iscariot, who became a traitor.
LUKE 6:12–16

Just prior to this time, the Pharisees had chided the Lord Jesus Christ that His followers walked through a grain field on the Sabbath, picking the heads of grain. They considered this working on the Sabbath, claiming that God forbid any labor.

The Pharisees had established thirty-nine books of Sabbath rules. Men interpreted what God meant instead of just obeying what God said.

These religious leaders became "filled with rage, and discussed together what they might do to Jesus" (Luke 6:11). What audacity! The God of the Creation, and initiator of the Sabbath, stood before them. And instead of listening and responding to Him, they thought to still His voice.

So Christ prayed all night for the men who would preach, teach, heal the sick, raise the dead, and record His Words. Christ chose a solitary spot, minimizing His distractions. When it's time to do battle we need to be alone first. Then, after we know God's will, we can solicit the prayers and fellowship of others.

Lord, Thank You for letting me come to You with all my
burdens, large and small. Only You can give true and
lasting peace.

OUR TRIUNE GOD

"Hear, O Israel! The Lord is our God, the Lord is one!"
DEUTERONOMY 6:4

Shema Yisroel Adonai Elohenu Adonai Echad is Hebrew for "'Hear, O Israel! The Lord our God is one Lord.'" That one verse illustrates why many Jews can't grasp the concept of the Trinity. The three distinct personalities that comprise the Trinity are all equal within the Godhead: Father, Son, and Holy Spirit. But the word "one" here should be interpreted as in a marriage context when the "two become one."

The Bible begins by letting the Jew know that this is true. Genesis 1:1 states, "In the beginning God created the heavens and the earth." The Hebrew word for "God" here is Elohim, a masculine plural noun. Thus the door to a doctrine of plurality in the Godhead is kicked wide open. When God speaks of Himself the plural pronoun is used: "Then God [Elohim] said, 'Let us make man in Our image, according to Our likeness'" (Genesis 1:26). All three persons of the Trinity were present.

Throughout the Scriptures there are references to the contributions of this Triune God while the Father spoke from heaven, confirming Christ at His baptism, the Holy Spirit descended upon Christ as a dove (John 1:31–34; Matthew 3:14–17).

Only God could have omnisciently conceived of the Trinity. God has always been, and will forever be.

Lord, I rejoice in my wonderful Savior, the Father who sent Him, and the Holy Spirit who gives me insight to understand Scripture.

The Original "Me Generation"

*And He called the twelve together, and gave them power
and authority over all the demons, and to heal diseases.
And He sent them out to proclaim the kingdom of God,
and to perform healing. And He said to them, "Take
nothing for your journey, neither a staff, nor a bag,
nor bread, nor money; and do not even have two tunics
apiece. And whatever house you enter,
stay there until you leave that city.*
LUKE 9:1–3

Remember what it was like as a kid to dream about having unlimited powers? Such fantasies have inspired cartoonists to create a variety of superheroes. In our hearts we know that these superheroes aren't real men and women. Human beings, if nothing else, are full of flaws, phobias, and fears.

He instructed His apostles not to take any possessions or provisions with them. Jesus wanted them to learn to rely fully on Him. But their lack of faith rendered them too weak to exercise this authority.

These were the men Christ had trained, empowered, and prepared to bring the Gospel message first to the Jews and then the Gentiles. They had been with Christ on a daily basis, learning from His example how to reach out with compassion to those in need. But instead they displayed both selfishness and a lack of love. How could they be left in charge of disseminating the Gospel? And yet they were God's Plan A.

Lord, how grateful I am that Your Holy Spirit worked in the lives of these apostles, molding them into strong men of faith. Help me to become unselfish with my time that many more will hear the Gospel.

A Call to Holiness

Our two sons easily tire of most board games. But they became immediately fascinated after one of their friends introduced them to the role-playing game Dungeons and Dragons. While our older son got a part-time job, which severely limited his free time, his younger brother went deeper and deeper into this seductive game.

About the same time, our church encouraged adults and high schoolers to sign up for the seminar "Basic Youth Conflicts." By the time the concluding all-day Saturday session rolled around, each one of us had been convicted by the Holy Spirit concerning our own "pet sins." All the way home that last evening our younger son spoke about how the game had usurped the time he used to spend with the Lord. He'd even begun feeling a strange sense of power come over him.

We watched as he pulled out a metal trash can and burned every one of the game's expensive books. From that moment Jeff never looked back.

Is God receiving all the glory in your life?

Lord, You know better than I what things will draw my time and attention away from You. Give me the courage to obey You.

MOSES IS IN GLORY

And behold, two men were talking with Him; and they
were Moses and Elijah, who, appearing in glory,
were speaking of His departure which He was
about to accomplish at Jerusalem.
LUKE 9:30–31

In case you've been feeling sorry for Moses who never got to enter the Promised Land, just look at what God had in store for him. These verses tell us that Moses and Elijah appeared in glory. But what does that really mean?

We are not now what we will become. For whether we die or are taken up by what is referred to as the Rapture, the Lord will someday allow this "earthsuit" of ours to fall away and issue us our "eternity suit."

"For if we believe that Jesus died and rose again, even so God will bring with Him those who have fallen asleep in Jesus. . .For the Lord Himself will descend from heaven with a shout, with the voice of the arch-angel, and with the trumpet of God; and the dead in Christ shall rise first. Then we who are alive and remain shall be caught up together with them in the clouds to meet the Lord in the air, and so we shall always be with the Lord" (1 Thessalonians 4:14, 16–17).

That day on top of the mountain, at Jesus' Transfiguration, the apostles witnessed Christ's glory and saw Moses and Elijah. And God spoke from the cloud which encompassed them saying, "'This is my Son, whom I have chosen; listen to Him'" (Luke 9:35).

In spite of your life, are you assured of your salvation?

Oh Lord, I am so grateful that my place with You is already reserved!

A Rock of Refuge

*Be to me a rock of habitation, to which I may continually
come; You have given commandment to save me,
For You are my rock and my fortress.*
PSALM 71:3

For several months before I attended my first writers'
conference in southern California I worked feverishly
compiling a manuscript for a book. However, when
an editor at the conference looked it over he told me
that it needed work. Being new to the field of writing,
his remarks devastated me.

I sought solace upon a large rock situated beside
a small lake. Tears of disappointment streaked down
my cheeks and as others approached I began walking.
I happened to encounter a bronze plaque that stated
the well-known evangelist, Billy Graham, had also
found peace in this place.

As the sun warmed that beautiful, tranquil setting, I considered another psalm about the Rock. "Be
to me a rock of strength, A stronghold to save me. For
You are my rock and my fortress; for Your name's sake
You will lead me and guide me" (Psalm 31:2–3).

Over fifty times in Scripture the word rock is
used in reference to God. When everything else fails,
He is steadfast, immovable, and unchangeable.

*Lord, You remain that Rock on which my faith stands
firm. How grateful I am that You uplift my spirit, that
You desire to use my talents. To God be the Glory!*

Martha and Mary

A woman named Martha welcomed Him into her home.
She had a sister called Mary, who was seated at the Lord's
feet listening to His word. But Martha was distracted with
all her preparations; and she came up to Him, and said,
"Lord, do You not care that my sister has left me to do
all the serving alone? Then tell her to help me."
Luke 10:38–40

Isn't this just how we feel when the men in our household excuse themselves from the table as soon as the first dirty dish appears? Martha, ever the perfect hostess, was left to do all the work. It didn't seem fair. However, what Martha really desired was a release from her compulsive neatness. And that's when the Lord presented her with a process for "chilling out."

"'Martha, Martha, you are worried and bothered about so many things; but only a few things are necessary, really only one, for Mary has chosen the good part, which shall not be taken away from her'" (Luke 10:41–42). In other words, all the busyness that now preoccupied Martha didn't really matter. Jesus was here and she was passing up a tremendous opportunity to learn from Him.

After all, who knew better than Christ how to put the pressures of life into perspective? He had only three years in which to establish His ministry, train up His disciples, and present the Gospel. Yet we see no record of Him hurrying others or running at a frantic pace.

Have you taken time to get to know your Lord? Perhaps your life, like Martha's, is missing the best part.

Lord, I pray for peace today from my busy schedule so I may learn at Your knee.

The Lord of Parables

*Listen, O my people, to my instruction; Incline your ears
to the words of my mouth. I will open my mouth in a
parable; I will utter dark sayings of old, Which we have
heard and known, And our fathers have told us.*
PSALM 78:1–3

Perhaps every family passes on their wise old sayings. My own was certainly no exception. For instance, "Many are cold but few are frozen," was my Irish father's Midwestern, change of season, winter's-bearing-down-on-us witticism.

Not to be outdone, my mother contributed such gems as, "Feed a cold, starve a fever!" We've handed down these tidbits to our own children, and no doubt they'll continue in some form for generations to come.

Christ did not dabble in nonsense. But sometimes Jesus offered His perfect insight in parables, or through stories with hidden meanings. "'To you it has been granted to know the mysteries of the kingdom of God, but to the rest it is in parables, in order that seeing they may not see, and hearing they may not understand'" (Luke 8:10).

Jesus had just shared with them the parable about the sower and the seed. He knew that those whose hearts were open and receptive to Him would understand its meaning. On the other hand, those whose hearts held only antagonism, jealousy, and self-righteousness would not understand even if He spoke plainly.

Is your heart ready to listen to Jesus?

When you examine the content of my heart, Lord, which type of soil have I prepared for Your Word?

JOSHUA IS CHOSEN

*"Be strong and courageous, for you shall go with this
people into the land which the Lord has sworn
to their fathers to give them, and you shall
give it to them as an inheritance."*

DEUTERONOMY 31:7

The family matriarch has died, and in the lawyer's
chambers, where the will is about to be unveiled, her
nearest and dearest huddle uncomfortably. And then
the lawyer announces the names of the recipients.
Suddenly those inheriting little turn to spew indigni-
ties on those receiving much. How often have we seen
this scenario played out in old movies?

Yet God did not allow those who taunted Moses
to challenge the authority of his successor. Moses,
who is preparing to die, names Joshua as his successor. Right there, in the presence of all Israel, Moses
admonishes Joshua to "'be strong and courageous.'"
God chose Joshua because he had faithfully served
Moses throughout all their years in the wilderness.

With his last bit of energy Moses recited the words
of the song God had given to him (Deuteronomy
32:1–27, NIV). "'Listen, O heavens, and I will speak;
hear, O earth, the words of my mouth, let my teaching fall like rain and my words descend like dew, like
showers on new grass, like abundant rain on tender
plants. . .'" and then it continues for forty-one more
verses. Please take time to read it all.

*Lord, I forget sometimes that those in leadership are chosen
by you. And with responsibility comes accountability.*

Spare the Rod

He who withholds his rod hates his son,
But he who loves him disciplines him diligently.
PROVERBS 13:24

As new parents, my husband and I couldn't imagine ever needing to discipline our little son. We anticipated that stating a pleasant no would result in immediate compliance. Wrong! Our little progeny had a mind of his own, and nothing would dissuade or cut short his determined purpose.

Our second son arrived with that compliant personality we'd joyfully anticipated the first time around. However, when the third one, a daughter, entered the world, we just threw up our arms in surrender!

The day I broke a worn-out wooden spoon while spanking our son was the day I invested in what later became "affectionately" known as "the lion paddle." About one inch thick, it covered their whole southern exposure when applied properly, and for the time being, resulted in better behavior. Until, that is, the lion paddle conveniently—and divinely—disappeared.

I believe nothing happens by chance. During this time I had become a born-again Christian. And not coincidentally, I had discovered that the fastest way to "redirect" my children's beastly actions was to require an immediate "kindness" as retribution to the injured party. At last I understood that "discipline" is meant to teach the correct behavior. "Punishment" only makes a child bitter.

Lord, help me to remember what Ann Ortland teaches,
that children are like wet cement. Assist me in making
good impressions in their lives.

A Willing Heart

"Jerusalem, Jerusalem, you who kill the prophets and stone those sent to you, how often I have longed to gather your children together, as a hen gathers her chicks under her wings, but you were not willing."
LUKE 13:34, NIV

I hate to bore you by rattling on about diets, so please "indulge" me for a few moments. I struggled for several months, attempting to obtain "abstinence." Yet it remained as illusive as grasping a cloud. My problem? I wasn't willing to let God take control.

Finally, as I obediently worked the first three steps of the Overeaters Anonymous program, peace followed. I admitted to being powerless because the compulsion to eat had made my life unmanageable. And I came to believe that God's power could restore me to sane eating. Then I made a decision to turn my will and life over to the Lord's care. And the "gift" of dietary abstinence became a part of my life.

This was actually the first time I realized that God was truly Almighty. When He made it easy for me to walk through life without being controlled by food, I knew He was real.

How like the Israelites I am! God showed them the path they were to walk in. He even defined the boundaries for them. And yet time after time they leaped beyond the lines of safety and tried to live without Him.

Is it time for you to let God steer the course?

Lord Almighty, whatever I desperately need release from today, please show me that You're able to heal as long as my heart is willing.

The God of Our Salvation

*Help us, O God of our salvation, for the glory of Your
name; And deliver us, and forgive our sins,
for Your name's sake. Why should the nations say,
"Where is their God?" Let there be known among the
nations in our sight, Vengeance for the blood
of Your servants, which has been shed.*

PSALM 79:9–10

God swore to Israel that He loved them. Now David
calls upon the Lord to forgive the people, knowing full
well that their present troubles directly correspond to
their disobedience.

Have you ever cried out to God for deliverance,
recognizing that your own circumstances are a direct
result of leaving the Lord out of the decision making?
We've all been there at one time or another. But God's
not surprised. He's not only aware of what we've done,
He watched us make this awful choice and then witnessed the harm we did to ourselves and others.

However, David recognized that if He didn't
"own his sin" and ask forgiveness from His Lord, there
was absolutely no hope of new beginnings.

In the New Testament, when Jesus asked the
Pharisees whose Son they thought Christ was, they
answered, "'The Son of David.'" In Matthew 22:43–
45: "[Jesus] said to them, 'Then how does David in the
Spirit call Him "Lord," saying, "The Lord said to my
Lord, 'Sit at My right hand, until I put Your enemies
beneath Your feet'"? If David then calls Him 'Lord,'
how is He his son?'" Jesus quoted Psalm 110:1, helping them understand that as God, Messiah is David's
Lord. And as man, He is David's son.

*We thank You that we can come to You as Lord and
Messiah. You are truly a God of forgiveness.*

God Uses Rahab

*Then Joshua the son of Nun sent two men as spies
secretly from Shittim, saying, "Go, view the land,
especially Jericho." So they went and came into the house
of a harlot whose name was Rahab, and lodged there.*
JOSHUA 2:1

When the king of Jericho found out that two Israelites
had snuck into town, he correctly assessed their intentions. These Israelite spies were investigating the land
so they could occupy it. Once Israel left Egypt, the
surrounding nations feared what would eventually
happen. So the king of Jericho sent word to Rahab, a
local prostitute, saying, "'Bring out the men who have
come to you, who have entered your house, for they
have come to search out all the land'" (Joshua 2:3).

Instead, Rahab hid Joshua's men on her roof, while
telling the king's soldiers they had already left the city.
Then she explained to Joshua's men: "'I know that the
Lord has given you the land, and that the terror of you
has fallen on us, and that all the inhabitants of the land
have melted away before you...for the LORD your God,
He is GOD in heaven above and on earth beneath'"
(Joshua 2:9–11).

Rahab then requested that when Joshua's men
conquered the city they would spare her life and also
that her family would be delivered from death. A red
cord dangling from the window of her house, the one
from which these men had escaped, would identify
her house as the one to be spared.

❧

Lord, how can You use me?

Heaven or Hell?

"Now there was a rich man. . .joyously living in splendor every day. And a poor man named Lazarus was laid at his gate, covered with sores, and longing to be fed with the crumbs which were falling from the rich man's table. . . Now the poor man died and was carried away by the angels to Abraham's bosom; and the rich man also died and was buried. And in Hades he lifted up his eyes, being in torment, and saw Abraham far away, and Lazarus in his bosom."
Luke 16:19–23

Jesus tells us what happened when two men died. During his lifetime, the rich man lavished in all the luxury this world had to offer. We know the love of God did not dwell in this man for he possessed no compassion for his fellow man. Instead of helping poor Lazarus, the rich man literally stepped over his dying body on his way out of the house. Certainly our all-knowing God correctly assessed the ugly selfishness of this wealthy man's heart.

In life each man chose the final direction his eternal soul would take. After death both are totally aware not only of their surroundings, but also of the great chasm that exists between them. For although Lazarus (not the same man Christ resurrected) could see and recognize the rich man, he was unable to go to him. Once life has ceased we no longer have the power to change our eternal destination. And although he suffered in life, the poor man now resided in paradise.

Father, I thank You that my deeds will not be assessed, but rather the state of my heart. For I know Your beloved Son!

Twelve Stones

*"You shall, moreover, command the priests who are
carrying the ark of the covenant, saying, 'When you
come to the edge of the waters of the Jordan,
you shall stand still in the Jordan.'"*
JOSHUA 3:8

Joshua had gathered the people together, revealing the
Lord's words. Then the people left their tents and followed the priests who carried the ark of the covenant.
When they reached the banks of the Jordan the water
stopped flowing. . .and the nation of Israel crossed
over!

Standing on the other side of the Jordan River the
men of Israel now followed God's command, "'Take
up for yourselves twelve stones from here out of the
middle of the Jordan, from the place where the priests'
feet are standing firm, and carry them over with you,
and lay them down in the lodging place where you
will lodge tonight'" (Joshua 4:3). These stones represented each of the tribes of Israel. Piled up high, they
produced a visible monument as to the miracle God
performed.

The 40,000-man liberation force, fully equipped
for battle, then proceeded to cross the desert plains
of Jericho.

As the news spread of God's miracle, so had the
level of terror. Jericho was "locked down and secured"
behind its gates. But God instructed Israel's warriors
to march around the city for six days. No obstacle can
prevent God's plan from being realized!

*Lord, please pave my way with stones from You, stones
of dedication, perseverance, and compassion.*

CIRCLE OF FEAR

And the Lord said to Joshua, "See, I have given Jericho into your hand, with its king and the valiant warriors. You shall march around the city, all the men of war circling the city once. You shall do so for six days."
JOSHUA 6:2

God gave the Israelites an elaborate battle plan (Joshua 6:2–5). And you won't believe who led them all in battle!

"Now it came about when Joshua was by Jericho, that he lifted up his eyes and looked, and behold, a man was standing opposite him with his sword drawn in his hand, and Joshua went to him and said to him, 'Are you for us or for our adversaries?' And he said, 'No, rather I indeed come now as captain of the host of the LORD.' And Joshua fell on his face to the earth, and bowed down, and said to him, 'What has my lord to say to his servant?' And the captain of the LORD's host said to Joshua, 'Remove your sandals from your feet, for the place where you are standing is holy.' And Joshua did so" (Joshua 5:13–15).

This is the same Lord who appeared to Abraham at the Oaks of Mamre and announced that Abraham's descendants would become a great and mighty nation (Genesis 18:1–33).

And this is the same Lord who is waiting for you to come to Him each and every day. He's waiting to lift you higher than you ever thought possible.

Lord, I need to remember that You are the Lord who not only guarantees victory in the battle but draws up the winning strategy. Thank You for that assurance.

REBUKE THE SINNER

"Be on your guard! If your brother sins, rebuke him;
and if he repents, forgive him."
LUKE 17:3

Back in the 1950s, neighborhood accountability was a fact of life. Families took pride in raising their children properly. And on the rare occasion when someone's kid did act up, it was guaranteed that by suppertime the parents would already have heard about it through the neighborhood grapevine. Punishment was swift and commensurate with the crime.

Since my husband and I had both benefited from the same kind of environment, we agreed completely on how we'd raise our children. However, in the early 1970s, we realized that a whole new breed of parents had evolved. They lacked the faith and fortitude to be disciplined or to discipline their own children.

Their children grew up for the most part without spiritual guidance, morality, or goals.

It still takes the knowledge of Jesus Christ to redeem our world. Here Jesus admonished His disciples to "rebuke" their brothers if they've sinned. Why? Because sin is a progressive fall. And "real love" means intervening that we might get back on track.

Have you shared your love of Jesus with a neighbor? Pray today that God might open a door or window to your witness.

Lord, give me the courage to be honest so that children can experience the safety and security of proper boundaries.

ᴸIVING WITH A VIEW OF HEAVEN

How lovely are Thy dwelling places, O LORD of Hosts!
My soul longed and even yearned for the courts of the
LORD; My heart and my flesh
sing for joy to the living God.
PSALM 84:1–2

My husband and I recently met a man who was instrumental in negotiating the freedom of some of the US troops listed as MIAs in Laos and Vietnam. As he related the horrors of war and the intricacies of bargaining with foreign governments, I realized this man possessed an inner strength and peace that had elevated him above the level of the despairing situations he described. Finally, I acknowledged, "You have a view of heaven that keeps you moving forward, don't you?"

"Yes," he answered emphatically. "And that faith in what lies ahead provides the stability I need despite the sandy soil on which I've stood. For man's promises are nothing, but God's are real."

King David also had an eternal perspective. Israel constantly battled their enemies. How he must have longed for a lasting peace. But he had to settle for that little niche of peace he carved out for himself while pondering what heaven was like, anticipating the day he'd dwell with God. For the God of perfection created for Himself a place of eternal security.

What knowledge we have that God desires to share this incredible place with His imperfect creatures! Despite our sinful nature, God truly loves us with an eternal affection.

David accepted Your love for him, Lord. Help me to live in Your will so my life is a blessing to You.

TRUE AND LASTING JUSTICE

*"In a certain city there was a judge who did not fear
God, and did not respect man. And there was a widow
in that city, and she kept coming to him, saying,
'Give me legal protection from my opponent.' And for a
while he was unwilling; but afterward he said to himself,
'Even though I do not fear God nor respect man,
yet because this widow bothers me, I will give her legal
protection, lest by continually coming she will wear me out.'"*
LUKE 18:2–5

A few years ago, my brother, a hospital janitor who worked the night shift, was stabbed while emptying the trash behind the main building. The men who attempted to murder him, just to steal his wallet, were never caught.

But God has been good to my brother. Bitterness isn't in his vocabulary. He forgave his attackers even before he was discharged from the hospital. He knows that someday "the just judge" will rule on these men's lives.

Back in New Testament times judges held court in a traveling tent. Whether cases were considered or not depended upon the plaintiffs' ability to "gain the attention of the judges' attendants." This widow in today's Scripture already had three strikes against her. First, as a woman she had no priority standing in the court. Second, as a widow she didn't have a husband to fight for her in these legal proceedings. And finally, without the funds to pay for assistance she was without hope.

If you've been denied justice here on earth, you have a God who sees all and knows all. Justice will be served!

Lord, You alone judge rightly. You alone will administer to the guilty the punishment they truly deserve.

Idols of Their Own Making

There is none like you among the gods, O Lord;
Nor are there any works like yours. . .For you are great
and do wondrous deeds; you alone are God.
PSALM 86:8, 10

Although my husband hadn't been enthusiastic about taking our travel trailer to Mexico, he didn't want to disappoint our close friends. (Perhaps he figured out that the real reason for this trip was so my girlfriend and I could shop for unusual gift items.)

Pottery-lined aisles drew our interest to the back of one small, cluttered store. And then we saw the "idols." Demonic-looking figures, half-man, half-beast, were intricately carved in wood and stone. With a cold shiver running down our spines, my friend and I exited that store so quickly we probably left a trail of dust.

When men and women refuse to worship the true God they invariably end up trying to fashion one on their own. The reason is natural: We were all created with a "God-shaped void" inside our souls. The purpose of this void is to draw us to the Lord in commitment.

Satan applies every subversive tactic in his arsenal in order to dim our understanding of God's attributes. Therefore, it's up to us to find the truth to combat the evil one's lies. On the other hand, God is constantly guiding us in our search for knowledge and understanding.

Lord, You've given me an entire Bible to read so that
I might learn of Your love, concern, and compassion.
Develop in me that sensitivity to "hear the prompting of
Your Spirit" while You guide me toward the truth.

RIDING ON A DONKEY

"Go into the village ahead of you; there, as you enter
you will find a colt tied on which no one yet has ever sat;
untie it and bring it here if anyone asks you,
'Why are you untying it?' You shall say,
'The Lord has need of it.'"
LUKE 19:30–31

Jesus came to them, riding on a donkey, just as it had been prophesied. "Rejoice greatly, O daughter of Zion! Shout in triumph, O daughter of Jerusalem! Behold, your king is coming to you; He is just and endowed with salvation, Humble, and mounted on a donkey, Even on a colt, the foal of a donkey" (Zechariah 9:9).

But why a donkey? The reason is that He might present Himself to them as their humble servant and King. If He had ridden into Jerusalem on a horse, He would have presented Himself as a warrior, ready for battle. That horse is already prophesied for the end times.

"And I saw heaven opened, and behold, a white horse, and He who sat upon it is called Faithful and True; and in righteousness He judges and wages war" (Revelation 19:11).

Now don't confuse the rider of this second white horse with the white horse and rider of what is known as the "four horsemen of the apocalypse." He is not Christ. Later in the year, when we study the Book of Revelation in more depth, this will become clear.

Lord, thank You for all the "absolutes" of Scripture.
I believe You are exactly who You claim to be, God
Incarnate.

IN THE BEGINNING, CHRIST

In the beginning was the Word. . .and the Word was God.
JOHN 1:1

An elderly woman once lived next door to us whom everyone came to call "Aunt Esther." At ninety-one, Esther's spunky attitude drew people to her.

But the church she attended was nothing more than a cult of false teachers. These teachers presented a new spin on an old lie, saying Jesus Christ did not exist in the flesh but was instead spirit.

As true believers we know differently: "By this you know the Spirit of God: every spirit that confesses that Jesus Christ has come in the flesh is from God; and every spirit that does not confess Jesus is not from God" (1 John 4:2–3).

The apostle John was an eyewitness to the events he was inspired by God's Spirit to record for us. "What was from the beginning, what we have heard, what we have seen with our eyes, what we have looked at and touched with our hands, concerning the Word of Life—and the life was manifested, and we have seen and testify and proclaim to you the eternal life, which was with the Father and was manifested to us" (1 John 1:1–2).

Aunt Esther would sit and take a dose of the Bible, but she followed the Truth with a soul-poisoning gulp from her cult's own book. Over and over I recited the first three verses of John's Gospel to her. At the age of ninty-three she suffered a stroke. Knowing her death was imminent, I lay on the floor next to her bed, praying all through the night. When she died a day later she knew Christ as her Savior.

Lord, I am so grateful to You for taking all those who profess Your name to be with You!

THE WISE WOMAN BUILDS HER HOUSE

The wise woman builds her house,
But the foolish tears it down with her own hands.
He who walks in his uprightness fears the Lord,
But he who is crooked in his ways despises Him.
PROVERBS 14:1–2

Among the construction management graduates in our son's class from Cal Poly in San Luis Obispo was one young woman. Striving to succeed in this tough and competitive major, she adapted exceedingly well both academically and socially. Indeed, like the wise woman of Scripture, she learned all the intricacies of proper building techniques.

Every woman must understand God's "building codes" in order to strengthen her own household. The blueprints must be followed. From these a concrete foundation is laid. Likewise, how can a woman provide guidance within her home unless she first seeks wisdom from the Lord?

Next comes the framing. This skeletal structure furnishes the undergirding and strength to support the home. Prayer is just such a sustenance to the family.

Now the insulation is added within the walls. This corresponds to godly friends and church members who provide a cushion to bolster us during the storms of life.

Finally, color-coated stucco and trim put the finishing touches on the exterior of the house. Our family portrays a unique image within our neighborhood. And the love we have for each other reflects the love and worship given to God.

Lord, You are the Master Builder. To stay upright I must follow Your blueprints.

He Dwelt Among Us

And the Word became flesh, and dwelt among us,
and we beheld His glory, glory as of the only begotten
from the Father, full of grace and truth. . .No man has
seen God at any time; the only begotten God, who is
in the bosom of the Father, He has explained Him.
JOHN 1:14, 18

That phrase, "dwelt among us," means God took on the form of a human body, leaving the peace, security, and hope of heaven, and came to earth to become a model for men and women.

How do you teach children not to lie, cheat, or steal? By being an example before them of proper behavior. Jesus showed us by example what it means to lead a perfect life, despite the evil surrounding Him. "For we do not have a high priest who cannot sympathize with our weaknesses, but one who has been tempted in all things as we are, yet without sin" (Hebrews 4:15).

When Satan bombarded Christ during an intense time of temptation in the wilderness, Christ showed us how to repel such attacks successfully: through liberal use of the Word of God, prayer, and obedience.

Blaming Adam for initiating humans into the vicious cycle of sin doesn't get any of us off the hook. It's our nature to sin. And that's why we need a new nature.

This is exactly what Christ purchased for us on Calvary's cross, the right to be indwelt with the very Spirit of God. A fresh start, isn't that what all of us are seeking?

Lord, strengthen my faith today. Help me to overcome the evil one's daily temptations.

ISRAEL BREAKS THE COVENANT

*"I brought you up out of Egypt and led you into the land
which I have sworn to your fathers. . . .
But you have not obeyed Me."*
JUDGES 2:1–2

No sooner had the Israelites taken possession of their land than they forgot all the Lord's admonitions.

"Then the sons of Israel did evil in the sight of the LORD, and served the Baals, and they forsook the LORD, the God of their fathers, who had brought them out of the land of Egypt, and followed other gods from among the gods of the peoples who were around them" (Judges 2:11–12).

God's hand was now against them for choosing to worship idols instead of honoring Him. Discipline was required to bring them back. But God never stopped loving these people He'd chosen. "And when the LORD raised up judges for them, the LORD was with the judge and delivered them from the hand of their enemies all the days of the judge; for the LORD was moved to pity by their groaning because of those who oppressed and afflicted them" (Judges 2:18).

For a while the people followed the judges, but as soon as one of these leaders died, the Israelites sought out their idols again. So God left five enemy nations as strongholds within the region to test Israel's obedience to His commandments: "the five lords of the Philistines and all the Canaanites and the Sidonians and the Hivites who lived in Mount Lebanon, from Mount Baal-hermon as far as Lebo-hamath" (Judges 3:3).

*Lord, cleanse my soul and fill me with Your strength that
I might not backslide into the pit of disobedience again.*

A Discerning Woman

*Wisdom reposes in the heart of the discerning and even
among fools she lets herself be known.*
PROVERBS 14:33, NIV

Dorothy, a precious older woman, faithfully attended
my Bible study group each week despite the fact that
she suffered from congestive heart failure. She was the
kind of person one treasured as a gift, knowing the time
with her would be all too brief. She shared the con-
tents of her heart freely, no longer restricted behind the
confining walls of decorum. From her perspective, the
word cherish didn't exist in her husband's vocabulary.

We would pray and cry together over the grief
her marriage had caused her soul. And then she'd sit
and play a beautiful hymn on the piano. This is the
way the Lord ministered to her pain. Confident of
her eternal destination, she exuded serenity, wisdom,
peace, and love. And the Lord called her home that
year because He valued her tremendously. She's buried in a cemetery near my house and I smile when I
pass by, knowing she's found a refuge where the music
never stops and people never cry.

Today's proverb says that, "wisdom reposes in the
heart of the discerning." How well Dorothy understood this. And although she couldn't change her
husband's heart, her own was filled with wisdom.
She'd learned the art of holding life like a kite, giving
it enough room to float freely and then watching as it
returned to her.

*Lord, everyone has a cross to bear. But because you bore
Calvary's cross for me, I have the hope of eternal life.*

ELIJAH WILL COME

And they asked him, "What then? Are you Elijah?"
And he said, "I am not."
JOHN 1:21

Around 433 BC God spoke through the prophet
Malachi, whose name means "My messenger." In the
first part of his prophecy Malachi writes, "'Behold,
I am going to send My messenger, and he will clear
the way before Me. And the Lord, whom you seek,
will suddenly come to His temple; and the messenger
of the covenant, in whom you delight, behold, He is
coming,' says the LORD of hosts" (Malachi 3:1).

The second part of Malachi's prophecy reveals
this: "'Behold, I am going to send you Elijah the
prophet before the coming of the great and terrible
day of the LORD. And he will restore the hearts of the
fathers to their children, and the hearts of the children to their fathers, so that I will not come and smite
the land with a curse'" (Malachi 4:5–6). For over four
hundred years after these words God was silent. No
wonder the Israelites were anxious to find out if John
the Baptist were the promised Elijah.

Clearly, John answers the Jews, saying that he is
not Elijah. However, he did come in the spirit and
power of Elijah and even dressed as Elijah had. John
preached a message of judgment for the religious
leaders of Israel who should have both known and
understood the Word of God but refused to listen.

Father, Jesus and John the Baptist delivered the truth of
Your Word but people refused to heed their messages.
Lord, help me to listen and respond.

Motives of the Heart

The plans of the heart belong to man, But the answer of the tongue is from the LORD. All the ways of a man are clean in his own sight, But the LORD weighs the motives. Commit your works to the LORD, And your plans will be established. The LORD has made everything for its own purpose, Even the wicked for the day of evil.
PROVERBS 16:1–4

Horoscopes in newspapers and psychic telephone hotlines exist because people have a natural curiosity to know the future. Despite the phenomenal success of recent Hollywood blockbusters, I can assure you an attack by aliens is not on the horizon. No, our real threat will come from within the very real but unseen spiritual realm, not the extraterrestrial.

You've heard the expression, "Men are from Mars and women are from Venus." But the Bible does not distinguish between the hearts of men and women: "The heart is more deceitful than all else And is desperately sick; Who can understand it?" (Jeremiah 17:9)

Surrounding us are beings from another world, but they belong to Satan. And their sole purpose is to seduce us into wavering from the truth. They dangle and then entangle us from the scaffolding of unbelief. Did God mean what He said? Doesn't He want us to have any fun? Do we really need Him telling us what to do? Absolutely! Only God can give us a secure, peaceful, and perfect future. An eternal future in heaven with Him.

Lord, there have been times when I compromised the truth of Your Word. Please help me get back on track. Place my feet firmly on the pavement of Your Word.

Adonai, My Lord

The LORD says to my LORD: "Sit at My right hand;
Until I make Your enemies a footstool for Your feet,"
The Lord will stretch forth Your strong scepter from
Zion, saying, "Rule in the midst of Your enemies."

PSALM 110:1–2

Unless you know that the Hebrew word Adonai refers to God alone, it's easy to misinterpret this passage. Who's having this conversation?

We know that God represented Himself by the use of the plural pronouns "us" and "our." "'Let Us make man in Our image, according to Our likeness'" (Genesis 1:26).

It's obvious that David understands the mystery of the Trinity and calls his Messiah God, Adonai, recognizing his Savior's equality with God the Father. This one passage represents two of the personalities within the Godhead.

David's Messiah was Jesus Christ, the son of David, his Savior from eternity past. And the answer as to who was speaking in Psalm 110 is provided as we read the cross-reference in the Gospel of Matthew. Jesus asked the Pharisees, "'What do you think about the Christ, whose son is He?' They said to Him, 'The son of David.' He said to them, 'Then how does David in the Spirit call Him "Lord," saying, "The Lord said to my Lord, 'Sit at my right hand, Until I put Your enemies beneath Your feet'"? If David then calls Him 'Lord,' how is He his son?' No one was able to answer Him a word, nor did anyone dare from that day on ask Him another question" (Matthew 22:41–46).

Father, I thank You that I can call You many names,
and all of them are beautiful and holy.

Finding the Messiah

He found first his own brother, Simon,
and said to him, "We have found the Messiah"
(which translated means Christ).
John 1:41

I'll never forget the day that I accepted Jesus Christ as my Savior. I'd been drawn to church twice that day, aware that my soul ached for peace. So many Christians had told me that all I needed to do was "pray and ask Christ into my life." But that seemed overly simplistic. How could this action change my life?

A short time before, while recovering from a compression fracture in my back, I began attending a Bible study. Now those Scriptures I'd heard there began to come back to me. It wasn't a matter of reciting words. Instead, asking Christ into my life meant being willing to trade all the emptiness and estrangement within my soul for the completeness He alone could provide.

At the age of twenty-nine, on Father's Day, I prayed to receive Christ, relinquishing control of my life to the Lord.

Andrew, speaking in today's Scripture, also found the Messiah and couldn't wait to tell his brother, Peter. That's how we all feel when God's light is at last turned on inside the dungeon of our souls.

How blessed for Andrew that his brother responded and they shared the love of the Lord together. In many families this never happens. Perhaps in reading this you understand what it means to be ridiculed because of your faith in Christ.

Lord, I pray for strength to share Your love with unbe-
lieving family members.

The Stone the Builders Rejected

*The stone which the builders rejected
Has become the chief corner stone.*
PSALM 118:22

When a building is started, a cornerstone must be placed precisely, because the rest of the structure is lined up with it. Likewise, Jesus Christ is the cornerstone of the Church. And His church is comprised of both Jews and Gentiles, united as the Body of Christ and dependent upon Him for guidance.

Before the world began, God envisioned His Church. Jesus Christ, the Son, would come and die for its members, that they would be cleansed from sin. And Christ would be the very foundation upon which this Church would stand. "'Where were you when I laid the foundation of the earth? Tell Me, if you have understanding, who set its measurements? Since you know. Or who laid its cornerstone, when the morning stars sang together, and all the sons of God shouted for joy?'" (Job 38:4–7).

But long before Christ came on the scene in recorded history, God prepared the Jews to accept their Messiah as the "cornerstone." Each year, as they celebrated the Feast of Passover they sang this psalm. And when Jesus, the chief cornerstone of God's mighty edifice, His kingdom, was in their very midst these melodious tones were sung by Him.

Is Jesus Christ the true cornerstone of your church? If you're looking for a church home, make sure you check the "foundation" first.

Lord Jesus Christ, You alone are to be the cornerstone of my life. Please help me to discard those concerns that block my view of You.

God's Protection for Widows

The Lord will tear down the house of the proud,
But He will establish the boundary of the widow.
PROVERBS 15:25

Christmas shopping preoccupied my father's thoughts as he picked out one special gift for each child, something he or she had wanted all year. But just after the last gift had been purchased, a severe heart attack overtook my dad. Although he was rushed to the hospital adjacent to the shopping center, he died almost immediately.

My mother's first concern was how she might continue caring for her children, all ten of whom lived at home. Although she hadn't worked outside the home in years, Mom donned a beret and smock, and began selling pastel portraits at the local swap meet.

Eventually Mom also filled artists' chairs at Knotts Berry Farm and the Movieland Wax Museum. Her beautiful pastel portraits still hang in homes throughout our area. And the friendships she made with other artists endure to this day.

No matter what her hardships, Mom has honored God, in whom she placed her faith and the care of her life. She's now been widowed far longer than the years she was married. She's raised her children, paid off her mortgage, and passed down her love of art to all her grandchildren.

Father, let me share Your Word with those women who now find themselves alone—"Now she who is a widow, indeed, and who has been left alone, has fixed her hope on God and continues in entreaties and prayers night and day" (1 Timothy 5:5).

An Angel Visits Ophrah

*Then the angel of the Lord came and sat under the oak
that was in Ophrah. . .Gideon was beating out wheat in
the wine press in order to save it from the Midianites.
And the angel of the Lord appeared to him and said to
him, "The LORD is with you, O valiant warrior."*
JUDGES 6:11–12

The Lord was about to sell a very surprised man
named Gideon on the idea of becoming Israel's next
judge. God knew Gideon longed for deliverance for
Israel. Once again Israel had turned to their age-old
sin of idolatry.

Gideon said to the Lord, "'O my lord, if the Lord
is with us, why then has all this happened to us? And
where are all His miracles which our fathers told us
about, saying, "Did not the Lord bring us up from
Egypt?" But now the Lord has abandoned us and
given us into the hand of Midian'" (Judges 6:13). For
once again the Israelites were enslaved as a result of
disobedience.

"And the Lord looked at him and said, 'Go in
this your strength and deliver Israel from the hand of
Midian. Have I not sent you?'" (Judges 6:14)

Have you ever felt that the weight of the world
rested on your shoulders? Well, that's Gideon for you.
"'O Lord, how shall I deliver Israel? Behold, my family is the least in Manasseh, and I am the youngest in
my father's house'" (Judges 6:15). The Lord answered
Gideon with the same resounding message of assurance which He always gives to His servants: "'Surely I
will be with you'" (Judges 6:16). God is with us in the
fight and that's enough!

Father, hold my hand today and every day.

100

MARY REQUESTS CHRIST'S HELP

"They have no wine."
JOHN 2:3

Jesus and His earthly mother Mary are guests at a wedding celebration in Cana, a celebration that suddenly becomes dimmed by a crisis. To run out of wine at such an event would have brought great shame on the host family, as in those days a wedding feast went on for an entire week. Mary's tender heart couldn't allow her friends to suffer such humiliation. At no time did she attempt to tell Christ what to do. She simply appealed to His inborn kindness and resourcefulness.

Christ's response is a statement of fact. "'Woman, what do I have to do with you? My hour has not yet come'" (John 2:4). Jesus was not yet ready to declare publicly to Israel His true identity. And performing an astonishing miracle would undoubtedly draw unwanted attention, as well as detract from the bride and groom.

But Mary had risked her very life for Him. When she was betrothed to Joseph, God sent an angel to ask her to bear the Messiah. She responded in obedience, and the Holy Spirit placed this child in the virgin's womb (Luke 1:26–35). An angel also appeared to Joseph, telling him that the child Mary had conceived was the Messiah (Matthew 1:18–25). But the scandal persisted. Jews were referred to as the son of their father. In Christ's case, people called Him "the son of Mary." Yet she'd accepted this indignity for Him. How could Christ possibly deny her the favor she asked? Confident of His intervention, Mary admonishes the servants, "'Whatever He says to you, do it'" (John 2:5).

Father, You are still the God of miracles. I thank You that You know my needs.

Knowing God's Precepts

Teach me Your statutes. Make me understand the way
of Your precepts, So I will meditate on Your wonders.
My soul weeps because of grief; Strengthen me according
to Your word. Remove the false way from me,
And graciously grant me Your law.
Psalm 119:26–29

Have you ever felt as if you've reached the end of the road and the only choice ahead of you is a brick wall? When you reach that point, the only remedy is to look up! God is waiting for you to come to your senses.

In these verses we learn the principles that can set things right. The first, revival, occurs when we truly "seek the Lord with all our hearts." Martin Luther, an Augustinian monk, recognized that the precepts he learned from studying the Scriptures didn't mesh with the teachings of the Roman Catholic Church. Therefore, in 1517, he openly stated his objections to the Catholic Church by nailing his Ninety-five "Theses" to the door of the church at Wittenberg. This began the revival that led to the formation of the Protestant church.

Confession of sin is the beginning of true hope. For when we acknowledge that we've failed, God can use our broken and contrite hearts, through the Holy Spirit, to mold us anew.

Understand and walk in the way of the precepts by meditating on God's Word. If you're not participating in an in-depth Bible study, consider finding or starting one.

Lord, teach me Your ways, that I might live out Your precepts before my family and loved ones.

A Great Teacher

"Truly, truly, I say to you, unless one is born again, he cannot see the kingdom of God."

JOHN 3:3

Nicodemus came to Christ under cover, by night. Although the Pharisees, the group of religious leaders to which he belonged, had reached the conclusion that Christ was sent from God, they hadn't bridged the gap to full understanding. Instead, they stood on the shore of uncertainty. They not only read the Scriptures, they taught them. And yet they bypassed the obvious and miraculous fulfillment to all the prophecies.

Note the timing of this visit by Nicodemus. The celebration of Passover was going on, and Jesus had just cleansed the temple of those who were, in His words, "'making My Father's house a house of merchandise'" (John 2:16).

Nicodemus obviously heard what Christ said and couldn't shake it loose from his thoughts. He sought the truth, so Christ made it as clear as a starlit night.

Later in the Scriptures we see Nicodemus as the one who boldly risks his life to help Joseph of Arimathea take Christ's body from the cross. And Nicodemus brought an expensive "mixture of myrrh and aloes, about a hundred pounds weight" (John 19:39). "So they took the body of Jesus and bound it in linen wrappings with the spices, as is the burial custom of the Jews" (John 19:40).

Lord, You told Nicodemus he must be born again. I praise You that You are the God of second chances, the God of truth!

Strength is Not in Numbers

And the LORD said to Gideon, "The people who are with you are too many for Me to give Midian into their hands, lest Israel become boastful, saying, 'My own power has delivered me.' Now therefore come, proclaim in the hearing of the people, saying, 'Whoever is afraid and trembling, let him return and depart from Mount Gilead.' "

JUDGES 7:2–3

Why can't we get it through our heads that if God is on our side, we don't need anyone else? Perhaps because we can't see Him.

Gideon had the same challenge. His own "battle strategy" included amassing a multitude that would obliterate the Midianites. And God told him no. God did not desire to perform a miracle that might be misconstrued as an act accomplished by human hands.

Instead, God had Gideon keep whittling down that number of troops. Finally, with a mere three hundred men Gideon crossed the Jordan and won the battle. But the people who followed him still hadn't understood.

These men said to Gideon, "'Rule over us, both you and your son, also your son's son, for you have delivered us from the hand of Midian'" (Judges 8:22). Gideon answered them, "'I will not rule over you, nor shall my son rule over you; the Lord shall rule over you'" (Judges 8:23).

Gideon served as Israel's judge for forty years and the land was undisturbed during that time. "Then it came about, as soon as Gideon was dead, that the sons of Israel again played the harlot with the Baals, and made Baal-berith their god" (Judges 8:33).

Lord, have I watched Your hand of deliverance in my own life only to become complacent? Help me repent!

FEARFULLY AND WONDERFULLY MADE

For You formed my inward parts; You wove me in my mother's womb. I will give thanks to You, for I am fearfully and wonderfully made; Wonderful are Your works, and my soul knows it very well. My frame was not hidden from You, When I was made in secret, And skillfully wrought in the depths of the earth. Your eyes have seen my unformed substance; And in Your book they were all written the days that were ordained for me, when as yet there was not one of them.

PSALM 139:13–16

Are you one of those people who picks up a new book and reads the last page first? Well, if your life could be compared to a book, only God knows the "ending" as well as the beginning. Despite the "pages" in the middle that might prove disappointing at times, God has a definite purpose for your life. And if you are in His will, the last page will have a very happy ending!

As we survey this "sea of humanity," we can feel as insignificant as a grain of sand. And yet one granule piled on top of another makes for a gorgeous beach.

Each of us has not only an inborn sense that there is a God, but also an understanding that we possess a designed intent. Your parents aren't responsible for your creation, God is. Had He not willed your very existence, you would not have happened. God wants to use your life to further His kingdom.

Lord, please renew my understanding that You created me in Your own image and likeness with a body, mind, and spirit.

ABSOLUTE ASSURANCE OF ETERNAL LIFE

"He who believes in the Son has eternal life;
but he who does not obey the Son shall not see life,
but the wrath of God abides on him."
JOHN 3:36

Rigo Lopez sought assurance one evening, alone in a motel room, as he surveyed the shattered pieces of his life. He'd just left his second wife and his children. Tears rolled down his cheeks, and he had no answers.

He turned on the TV, and by the grace of God, Billy Graham's voice carried to him a message of hope. "You can have absolute assurance today of your salvation," Graham preached. Those words became like a heat-seeking missile, going directly to the source of pain in Rigo's heart. Rigo then prayed, "God, give me that assurance. Help me to know that You can forgive me, make me whole, and salvage the ruins of my life."

Armed with this knowledge, Rigo returned home to his family and began again. He read, studied, and eventually taught the Bible to others. This is the point at which I came to know him, as a member of my church. For years he and his wife Nancy taught Sunday school. Yet even when Rigo was diagnosed with incurable cancer, these two faithfully continued at their post. He was only in his forties when God called him home. The large church contained so many mourners that many had to stand in the vestibule.

The Word of God says that we can have absolute assurance of eternal life today. Rigo grasped onto God's truth, and his life was transformed.

Lord, I am assured of my salvation. Help me share this absolute truth with those in despair.

An Arrogant King

And Abimelech the son of Jerubbaal went to Shechem to his mother's relatives, saying, "Speak now, in the hearing of all the leaders of Shechem, 'Which is better for you, that seventy men, all the sons of Jerubbaal, rule over you, or that one man rule over you?' Also, remember that I am your bone and your flesh."
JUDGES 9:1–2

After the death of Jerubbaal (Gideon), one of his own sons devised a plot to fill the power gap and become king.

"Then he went to his father's house at Ophrah, and killed his brothers the sons of Jerubbaal, seventy men, on one stone. But Jotham the youngest son of Jerubbaal was left, for he hid himself" (Judges 9:5).

Even knowing this man to be a murderer, the men of Shechem and the surrounding area gathered together and crowned Abimelech king.

Jotham called these people of Shechem to accountability, reminding them of how fairly they'd been treated by Gideon. When they refused to listen, he called for a curse from God upon them and escaped to Beer. The people chose to follow Abimelech for three years.

"Then God sent an evil spirit between Abimelech and the men of Shechem; and the men of Shechem dealt treacherously with Abimelech, in order that the violence done to the seventy sons of Jerubbaal might come" (Judges 9:23–24). The God of justice always intervenes to bring the course of history in line with His own design.

Lord, Your eyes see everything. You are a God of unswerving justice.

Encounter at the Well

So He came to a city of Samaria called Sychar. So near the parcel of ground that Jacob gave to his son Joseph; and Jacob's well was there Jesus, being wearied from His journey, was sitting thus by the well. It was about the sixth hour. There came a woman of Samaria to draw water. Jesus said to her, "Give Me a drink."

John 4:5–7

Here lived a woman of ill repute. Gathering water was a task customarily performed by the village women early in the day. Her presence at the well late in the afternoon was an acknowledgment that she didn't fit in. She was shunned by those who led wholesome lives. After all, she had had five husbands and now lived with a man.

Although men didn't speak to women in public, Jesus asked this woman for a drink of water. Shocked, the woman responded, "'How is it that You, being a Jew, ask me for a drink since I am a Samaritan woman?'" (John 4:9) No self-respecting Jew would stoop to address pagans.

Jesus Christ goes right to the heart of her problem. "'If you knew the gift of God, and who it is who says to you, 'Give Me a drink,' you would have asked Him, and He would have given you living water'" (John 4:10). And when she asked where to get this living water, He explained the process of eternal life to her.

Transformed, she ran back to town relating her amazing news: "'Come, see a man who told me all the things that I have done; this is not the Christ, is it?'" (John 4:29)

Father, help me to seek out those who for whatever reason are shunned and despised. They need You so much.

A Hasty Vow

*Now Jephthah the Gileadite was a valiant warrior,
but he was the son of a harlot. And Gilead was the father
of Jephthah. And Gilead's wife bore him sons; and when
his wife's sons grew up, they drove Jephthah out and said
to him, "You shall not have an inheritance in our father's
house, for you are the son of another woman."*
JUDGES 11:1–2

Two more judges led Israel following the death of Abimelech. Not surprisingly, the feckless Israelites once again began to serve the pagan Baals and Ashteroth.

Finally, the Israelites acknowledged their sin and cried out again for God's intervention. He chose Jephthah as their judge and his brothers came to him for deliverance. Victorious over many enemies, Jephthah made a vow to the Lord that if He would give them deliverance from the sons of Ammon, Jephthah would sacrifice a burnt offering to God of whatever came out of his house first, upon his return from battle.

Tragically, Jephthah's only child, a daughter, bounded out the front door to meet him "with tambourines and with dancing" (Judges 11:34). After her father explained the vow he'd just made, she said to him, "'My father, you have given your word to the Lord; do to me as you have said'" (Judges 11:36).

She was sacrificed, just as Jephthah had promised. "Thus the daughters of Israel went yearly to commemorate the daughter of Jephthah the Gileadite four days in the year" (Judges 11:39–40).

Lord, help me turn to You for my deliverance and not make hasty, costly vows.

All is Vanity!

The words of the Preacher, the son of David,
king in Jerusalem. "Vanity of vanities," says the Preacher,
"Vanity of vanities! All is vanity."
ECCLESIASTES 1:1–2

At the end of his life, King Solomon, who is thought to be the writer of Ecclesiastes, concludes that the things of earth are but fleeting. Perhaps you too are prone to reflect on the tasks that occupy your days, concluding that nothing gets accomplished.

From the very beginning my husband and I decided that I would stay home with the kids and he'd work to support us. We have always managed to own a home in a nice neighborhood, send our kids to good schools, and afford at least a summer "camping vacation."

At times I'd lust after the sumptuous decor of a neighbor's home or envy those who lived in the two-story homes in the adjacent tract. But we stayed put. Years later, I finally appreciated that "low mortgage" when we were able to refinance and send three kids to college.

As we go through Ecclesiastes, Solomon repeatedly uses two key word pictures, "meaningless" and "under the sun." As king over Israel he had seen "all the works which have been done under the sun, and behold, all is vanity and striving after wind...Because in much wisdom there is much grief, and increasing knowledge results in increasing pain" (Ecclesiastes 1:14, 18). Solomon had experienced the best the world has to offer...and it wasn't enough.

Lord, as I begin to learn the truths contained in this book, please help me view my priorities from Your perspective.

Healed Miraculously

Now there is in Jerusalem by the sheep gate a pool. . .
having five porticoes. In these lay a multitude of those
who were sick, blind, lame, and withered, (waiting for
the moving of the waters; for an angel of the Lord went
down at certain seasons into the pool, and stirred up
the water; whoever then first, after the stirring up of the
water, stepped in was made well from whatever
disease with which he was afflicted.)
John 5:2–4

So many times when we cry out to the Lord for healing, He seems to be asking us the same question He posed to the man who had been sitting at this gate for thirty-eight years waiting for healing: "'Do you wish to get well?'" (John 5:6)

In other words, do you honestly desire to rid yourself of the things that debilitate? For true healing of our souls requires a change of direction.

Evidently, this man had never asked for assistance in reaching the restorative waters. Instead, he just lay there day after day, on the fringe of what "could have been." A few verses later Jesus zeroes in on the core of the man's problem. "'Do not sin anymore'" (John 5:14).

Now everyone who is sick is not necessarily guilty of sin. Later, Christ is asked by the disciples whether or not a man sinned. Jesus answered, "'It was neither that this man sinned, nor his parents; but it was in order that the works of God might be displayed in him'" (John 9:3). Only God knows the content of one's heart.

Lord, if sin is at the root of my infirmity, then bring me to swift repentance. But if my suffering is to point others toward Your glory, quench my thirst with Your living water.

$\mathcal{U}$NREMARKABLE $\mathcal{L}$IVES

*Then Jephthah the Gileadite died and was buried in one
of the cities of Gilead. Now Ibzan of Bethlehem judged
Israel after him. And he had thirty sons, and thirty
daughters whom he gave in marriage outside the family,
and he brought in thirty daughters from outside
for his sons. And he judged Israel seven years.
Then Ibzan died and was buried in Bethlehem.*
JUDGES 12:7–10

What do you want etched into your own tomb-
stone? Personally, I'd like to be remembered this way:
"Studied the Word of God diligently and cared about
bringing it to others."

But no such accolades are recorded for the four
judges Jephthah, Ibzan, Elon, and Abdon. Jephthah is
known mainly for his "rash vow," while Ibzan's claim
to fame is a large family, whom he married off to the
pagans dwelling in that area. That's the route that led
to unbelief and pagan idolatry over and over during
the time in which the judges ruled Israel. Nothing is
learned about Abdon except that "he had forty sons
and thirty grandsons who rode on seventy donkeys"
(Judges 12:14). What other tangible effects of his
presence on earth did he leave behind?

How can we discern the will of God for our lives?
Daily prayer is definitely the main source. And this
involves not only relating our needs to God, but also
listening for His directions. For He never meant for
us to traverse through this maze called life without
the road maps He would supply.

*Lord, remind me to linger in prayer, listening for Your
voice.*

*J*ESUS, *B*READ OF *L*IFE

"As the living Father sent Me, and I live because of the
Father, so he who eats Me, he also shall live because of
Me. This is the bread which came down out of heaven;
not as the fathers ate, and died, he who eats
this bread shall live forever."
JOHN 6:57–58

Have you ever sat in a large lecture hall, listening to an
intellectual speaker who extended your mind past the
breaking point? Well, this is how the Jews of this day
reacted to Christ as He spoke these words to them.
They hadn't the vaguest notion as to how they might
apply this information. If their minds had been file
drawers, they'd have been in a quandary as to which
file category to place it all under.

These listeners knew what the Scriptures said
and yet they had no real comprehension that these
God-breathed words were being fulfilled before their
very eyes. So, they applied human understanding to
Christ's words.

Some said that Jesus' teachings were too difficult
to even bother with, while others stated that Christ
was speaking about cannibalism. But the major-
ity just walked away, refusing to follow Christ anymore. To continue following Him required faith and
commitment.

To truly partake of Christ is to accept Him as He
is, fully God and fully man, sent from God, recognizing our need for Him. He came first to the Jews, but
they refused the message. What is your response?

Lord, when I don't understand the Scriptures, Your
Holy Spirit will provide me with comprehension.

SAMSON IS CONCEIVED

*Then the angel of the LORD appeared to the woman,
and said to her "Behold now, you are barren
and have borne no children, but you shall
conceive and give birth to a son."*

JUDGES 13:3

Once again, God was about to raise up a deliverer for Israel. And the woman joyfully brought the news to her husband. "'A man of God came to me and his appearance was like the appearance of the angel of God, very awesome...He said to me, "Behold, you shall conceive and give birth to a son, and now you shall not drink wine or strong drink nor eat any unclean thing, for the boy shall be a Nazarite to God from the womb to the day of his death"'" (Judges 13:6–7).

From the moment of conception, Samson's mother was to abstain from alcohol. God didn't want Samson to be born with a dependence on alcohol: Samson's mind needed to be clear so that he could receive the Lord's direction and guidance to lead Israel.

Also, God made it clear to her that "from the moment of conception" this was in fact a son. No confusion here either. But abortion advocates tell us otherwise, despite the Lord's pronouncement that following the union of the sperm and egg, a unique human has been created. Truly the wisdom of the Lord defies time, technology, and human arrogance.

Lord, as I read Your Word, open my eyes to Your infinite wisdom and understanding.

Not Even His Brothers Believed

*Now the feast of the Jews, the Feast of Booths,
was near. Therefore His brothers said to Him,
"Leave here, and go into Judea, so that Your disciples also
may see Your works which You are doing. For no one does
anything in secret when he himself seeks to be known
publicly. If You do these things, show Yourself to the
world." For not even His brothers were believing in Him.*
John 7:2–5

One of the most difficult challenges any believer faces
is reaching her family with Christ's message. Although
Jesus' own brothers had daily viewed His sinless life, they
were as blind as the Pharisees to who He really was.

Surely these siblings, Christ's earthly half-
brothers (Matthew 13:55–56, Mark 6:1–6), knew
that the Jews were seeking to kill Him (John 7:1). But
they were headed for Jerusalem to attend the Feast
of Booths, as required by God. Jesus' brothers were
embarking on a journey to a religious feast and yet
rejecting their own Messiah.

Their unbelief had been prophesied in Psalm
69:8: "I have become estranged from my brothers,
And an alien to my mother's sons."

Christ's half-brothers were completely in tune
with the world, and not with God. Jesus tells them,
"'My time is not yet at hand, but your time is always
opportune. . .Go up to the feast yourselves; I do not
go up to this feast because My time has not yet fully
come'" (John 7:6–8). After his brothers left, Christ
went secretly to the feast.

*Thank You, Jesus, for reminding me to wait for God's
timing in my life, especially when the pressure applied by
others would have me rush on ahead.*

A Time to Mourn

There is an appointed time for everything.
And there is a time for every event under heaven...
A time to weep, and a time to laugh;
A time to mourn, and a time to dance.
ECCLESIASTES 3:1, 4

Once we've finally accepted that God truly loves us, it's hard to face the first discouraging episode or tragedy that follows. One young family had received a strong call from the Lord to the mission field. At the beginning of a fund-raising trip they were involved in an accident that totaled their van. What would they do? They transferred their focus away from the problem and to their faithful Lord who never disappoints.

Somehow we reach the faulty conclusion that if God loves us all negative incidents are nixed. Do we doubt that the Father loved the Son and yet allowed the Son to suffer a cruel death on the cross? The penalty for sin was death, a penalty that had to be paid by someone absolutely sinless in order for us to be forgiven. Only Jesus Christ could fill that role.

If Christ Himself suffered, then why should we be immune from all maladies?

Occasionally a time of mourning enters our lives, sometimes stealing in almost silently, sometimes brashly breaking down the door to our well-constructed sense of security. Neither path reflects nor distorts the fact that God loves us. But tragedy and mourning are both part of the ebb and flow or "rhythm of life."

Lord, through my veil of tears help me to view Your rescuing hand, that I might reach out to grasp You more firmly.

An Adulterous Woman

*The scribes and the Pharisees brought a woman caught
in adultery, and having set her in the center of the court,
they said to Him, "Teacher, this woman has been
caught in adultery, in the very act. Now in the
Law Moses commanded us to stone such women;
what then do You say?"*
John 8:3–5

What a scene! The Jewish religious leaders had
dragged this woman right out of bed. But where is
her partner in crime? Since Jewish law required that
both parties involved in this sin be stoned, it's a sham
from the beginning. It was staged by the Pharisees as
a trap for Jesus.

The Pharisees meant to pit Christ's ruling against
what Moses had commanded. However, their plot
backfired! "But Jesus stooped down, and with His
finger wrote on the ground" (John 8:6). At first they
blindly persisted in asking His opinion on this matter.

Then, "He straightened up, and said to them, 'He
who is without sin among you, let him be the first to
throw a stone at her.'" Had he etched out their sins
for all to read? We don't know for sure, but when He
stooped down to continue writing again, "they began
to go out one by one, beginning with the older ones,
and He was left alone, and the woman, where she had
been, in the midst" (John 8:7, 9).

"And straightening up, Jesus said to her, 'Woman,
where are they? Did no one condemn you?' And she
said, 'No one, Lord.' And Jesus said, 'Neither do I condemn you; go your way, from now on sin no more'"
(John 8:10–11).

*Lord, forgive me, no matter what my sin, that I might
turn from it and faithfully serve You.*

The Days of Your Youth

Remember also your Creator in the days of your youth,
before the evil days come and the years draw near when
you will say, "I have no delight in them." . . .Fear God
and keep His commandments, because this applies to
every person. For God will bring every act to judgment,
everything which is hidden, whether it is good or evil.

ECCLESIASTES 12:1, 13–14

Most of us have encountered women who freely share biblical truths "handed down to them" from their grandmothers or mothers. Is the faith being displayed in their lives?

The Book of Ecclesiastes concludes with the admonition not only to remember our Creator when we are young, but to continue following His precepts throughout our time on earth. For nothing is sadder than to see those who began the race of life with so much vigor and potential now sitting on the sidelines watching the parade pass by.

High school reunions are great places to witness such scenes. Those girls whose faces glowed with extraordinary promise at eighteen may now display ones that appear more like a map of New York City. They've been betrayed, besieged, and bewildered by people promising much and delivering little.

Have you forgotten the God of your youth? Have His principles been compromised away by the pressures of a world that teaches the Ten Commandments are optional? With the Lord's help, it's not too late to turn it all around.

Lord, if I look back and see a trail of regret, please give
me the courage to change the view.

Jesus, Light of the World

As He passed by, He saw a man blind from birth.
And His disciples asked Him, saying, "Rabbi, who
sinned, this man or his parents, that he should be born
blind?" Jesus answered, "It was neither that this man
sinned, nor his parents; but it was in order that the
works of God might be displayed in him."
JOHN 9:1–5

When you walk into a darkened room, you reach for the light switch. Back in Christ's time, you might have waited for the first rays of sunlight to break through the morning sky. However, for the man in today's Scripture that first glimmer of daily hope had never arrived. He'd been born blind.

But Jesus intervened. "He spat on the ground, and made clay of the spittle, and applied the clay to his eyes, and said to him, 'Go, wash in the pool of Siloam.' And so he went away and washed, and came back seeing" (John 9:6–7).

Some of the neighbors who had known the man as a beggar were astonished, while others doubted that he was even the same man.

Then the Pharisees brought in the man's parents, questioning them. And even when they heard the truth they refused to believe, becoming divided as to whether a mere man had performed a miracle. "Don't confuse us with the facts," they seemed to say.

Rather than believe that the man had actually been healed, the Pharisees once again donned their mask of spiritual blindness, threatening to excommunicate the man from temple worship. No miracle of God was about to shake up their world!

Lord, open my eyes to Your miracles.

RUTH, FAITHFUL DAUGHTER-IN-LAW

*Then Elimelech, Naomi's husband, died; and she was
left with her two sons. And they took for themselves
Moabite women as wives; the name of the one
was Orpah and the name of the other Ruth.
And they lived there about ten years.*

RUTH 1:3–4

Ruth was a young woman when her husband died.
In one of the greatest testaments of love in the Bible,
she chose to remain with her widowed mother-in-law,
Naomi, even choosing to believe in her God.

Naomi's encouragement that Ruth return to her
homeland only deepened Ruth's commitment to follow. "'Do not urge me to leave you or turn back from
following you; for where you go, I will go, and where
you lodge, I will lodge. Your people shall be my people, and your God, my God. Where you die, I will die,
and there I will be buried. Thus may the Lord do to
me, and worse, if anything but death parts you and
me'" (Ruth 1:16–17).

Few daughters-in-law would have persisted in
devotion to a woman whose life held such abysmal tragedy and so little prospect for positive change. However,
God had a glorious plan. "Now Naomi had a kinsman
of her husband, a man of great wealth, of the family of
Elimelech, whose name was Boaz" (Ruth 2:1).

Ruth gathered leftover grain from Boaz's fields
so that she and Naomi might have food. And Boaz
showed her favor. In time, Ruth would become Boaz's
bride and mother to his son, a son whose lineage
would include David and the Messiah, Jesus Christ.

Lord, may I learn from Ruth's example of abiding love.

120

Hannah's Prayer is Observed

She, greatly distressed, prayed to the Lord and wept bitterly. And she made a vow and said, "O Lord of hosts, if You will give indeed look upon the affliction of Your maidservant and remember me, and not forget Your maidservant, but will give Your maidservant a son, then I will give him to the Lord all the days of his life, and a razor shall never come on his head."
1 Samuel 1:10–11

Hannah has gone to the temple year after year and pleaded with God for a son. Her husband says, "'Hannah, why do you weep and why do you not eat and why is your heart sad? Am I not better to you than ten sons?'" (1 Samuel 1:8)

Eli the priest happened upon the scene. He had missed Hannah's heartfelt prayer. All he saw was her mouth moving. Eli concluded that Hannah was drunk and said, "'How long will you make yourself drunk? Put away your wine from you'" (1 Samuel 1:14).

But Hannah answered and said, "'No, my lord, I am a woman oppressed in spirit; I have drunk neither wine nor strong drink but I have poured out my soul before the Lord. Do not consider your maidservant as a worthless woman; for I have spoken until now out of my great concern and provocation'" (1 Samuel 1:15–16).

Finally, Eli did rally, giving Hannah a blessing, "'Go in peace; and may the God of Israel grant your petition that you have asked of Him'" (1 Samuel 1:17). The persistent prayers of a Christian woman should never be underestimated!

Lord, help me to realize that "our help is in the name of the Lord!" (Psalm 124:8).

THE SONG OF SOLOMON

"My beloved responded and said to me, 'Arise, my darling, my beautiful one, And come along. For behold, the winter is past, The rain is over and gone. The flowers have already appeared in the land; The time has arrived for pruning the vines, And the voice of the turtledove has been heard in our land. The fig tree has ripened its figs, And the vines in blossom have given forth their fragrance. Arise, my darling, my beautiful one, And come along!' "

SONG OF SOLOMON 2:10–13

Crucial to understanding the Scriptures is analyzing the composition or type of literature within each book of the Bible.

The Song of Solomon is a book of poetry. During the eighth day of Passover the Jews would sing portions of this book, which they compared to the most holy place in the temple.

Approaching this unique little book with the understanding that it's a love story enables the reader to appreciate its lyrical quality. Yet the Song of Solomon also addresses issues of pertinence to women. Understanding ourselves and our mates, the importance of intimacy and purity, and the concept of fidelity within the marital union are all discussed.

Most importantly, the Song of Solomon explores the spiritual relationship we have with God. In his letter to the church at Corinth (2 Corinthians 11:2), the apostle Paul also speaks to this issue. "For I am jealous for you with a godly jealousy; for I betrothed you to one husband, that to Christ I might present you as a pure virgin. Have you forsaken your first love?"

Lord, make me a woman who is faithfully devoted to You.

Jesus, the Good Shepherd

"He who enters by the door is a shepherd of the sheep.
To him the doorkeeper opens, and the sheep
hear his voice, and he calls his own sheep
by name, and leads them out."
John 10:2–3

Sheep just aren't very bright. They need constant overseeing, tender treatment, and strict boundaries. The shepherd took them to the best pastures, found safe lodging for them during the night, and then led them out again in the morning. He was the ultimate caregiver!

In fact, the shepherd would stretch his own body out across the opening to the sheep pen. What a graphic picture of protection this provides as we consider that Christ considers Himself our Shepherd.

As the world screams out for us to follow every wind of doctrine, Christ's voice calls us back to obedience: "'When he puts forth all his own, he goes before them, and the sheep follow him because they know his voice'" (John 10:4). His voice will never call us to rebellion, sinful pleasures, or departure from His Word.

In our day we hear those who defend heinous acts by saying, "Voices told me to do it." Certainly the one they chose to listen to was not the voice of Jesus Christ, for He cannot contradict Himself. True sheep listen only for the voice of their Shepherd.

God calls us by name, just as the shepherd has pet names for his sheep. Someday, when the King of Kings, our Good Shepherd, calls us home to heaven, we'll hear the name He calls us.

Lord, guide me to safe pastures today. Never leave me.

Samuel is Born

*It came about in due time, after Hannah
had conceived, that she gave birth to a son;
and she named him Samuel, saying, "Because
I have asked him of the Lord."*
1 Samuel 1:20

Hannah, a woman of real faith, wanted to keep her promise to God. After Samuel was born and she had weaned him, she took him promptly to the temple. There she said to Eli, "'Oh, my lord! As your soul lives, my lord, I am the woman who stood here beside you, praying to the Lord. For this boy I prayed, and the Lord has given me my petition which I asked of Him. So I have dedicated him to the Lord; as long as he lives he is dedicated to the Lord'" (1 Samuel 1:26–28).

Every year Hannah and Elkanah returned for their sacrifice at the temple, and every year Hannah brought Samuel a new robe to wear. For her faithfulness, God blessed Hannah with three more sons and two daughters (1 Samuel 2:21).

God was now training Samuel to take over as judge of Israel, as Eli's own sons had no regard for the Lord. As Samuel continued to grow "in favor with the Lord" (1 Samuel 2:26), the Lord declared, "'Those who honor me I will honor, but those who despise me will be disdained'" (1 Samuel 2:30 NIV).

Lord, If You should give me a child, guide me as You guided Hannah—to sincere faithfulness.

ISAIAH, A MAJOR PROPHET

The vision of Isaiah the son of Amoz concerning Judah
and Jerusalem, which he saw during the reigns of Uzziah,
Jotham, Ahaz, and Hezekiah, kings of Judah. Listen,
O heavens, and hear, O earth; for the LORD speaks,
"Sons I have reared and brought up, But they have
revolted against Me. . . . My people do not understand."
ISAIAH 1:1–3

Had the word "clueless" been coined during Isaiah's lifetime, he would probably have used it to describe the people of Israel who foolishly continued to abandon the Lord. However, through the prophet Isaiah, God provides extraordinary clues to His character. This prophet was surely named appropriately, for Isaiah means "Jehovah saves" or "salvation of Jehovah."

Isaiah's very lifeblood would be poured out as he brought this message of hope to Israel, for it is written that he was sawed in two by Manasseh, the king of Judah who reigned after Hezekiah (2 Kings 21:16).

Reading Isaiah provides a necessary heart check. Like Israel, if we fail to turn from our defiant ways, we must ask, "Where will you be stricken again, As you continue in your rebellion? The whole head is sick, And the whole heart is faint. From the sole of the foot even to the head there is nothing sound in it, Only bruises, welts, and raw wounds, Not pressed out or bandaged, Nor softened with oil" (Isaiah 1:5–6).

Lord, this book of prophecy displays Your promises and prophecies. Open my mind to receive Your truth. And keep me from confusion, that I might know You as both Messiah and Lord.

Jesus Raises Lazarus

Now a certain man was sick, Lazarus of Bethany. . .
The sisters sent to Him, saying,
"Lord, behold, he whom You love is sick."
JOHN 11:1, 3

When we hear that a good friend is critically ill, we run to his side. Why then does Jesus tarry? "But when Jesus heard it, He said, 'This sickness is not unto death, but for the glory of God, that the Son of God may be glorified by it'" (John 1:4).

Obviously, this remark puzzled His disciples. They had honestly laid out the situation for Him. Lazarus was about to breathe his last. And yet Christ seemed to be denying the gravity of the situation. We can almost picture Mary and Martha wringing their hands and consoling each other that soon Jesus would be there and everything would be all right again.

Instead, Jesus took His time getting there, four days as a matter of fact. And when He did arrive, Lazarus had been buried! Now Christ was only a few miles away from Bethany. It took all the human restraint He possessed not to run to Lazarus's aid. But Jesus has, as always, a greater purpose.

At the tomb of His friend Jesus called: "'Lazarus, come forth'" (John 11:43). And Lazarus arose from the tomb and walked out, his grave clothes dangling from his body. Have you allowed Christ to exercise His authority to bring you forth to new life?

Lord, strengthen my faith so that when tragedy strikes,
I know that You are the Resurrection and the Life.

HANNAH ACKNOWLEDGES HER SAVIOR

Then Hannah prayed and said, "My heart exults in the LORD; My horn is exalted in the LORD, My mouth speaks boldly against my enemies, Because I rejoice in Your salvation. There is no one holy like the LORD, Indeed, there is no one besides You, Nor is there any rock like our God. Boast no more so very proudly, do not let arrogance come out of your mouth; for the LORD is a God of knowledge, And with Him actions are weighed."
1 SAMUEL 2:1–3

Recently my husband and I toured William Randolph Hearst's castle in San Simeon, California. Surrounded by opulence and indulgence, embodied by his fabled art collection, Hearst had missed what was truly valuable—the reality of Christ's powerful light invading the darkness of one's sin-ridden soul.

Hannah, on the other hand, is very aware of the one truth of her life and she expresses it eloquently: "'I rejoice in Your salvation.'"

Hannah spent her time in the temple, praying and serving others. And God granted the deepest longing of her heart, despite the fact that she was just a sinner who could offer God nothing but her brokenness and yielded spirit.

Hannah refers to her Savior as a "'God of knowledge'" for she revered or honored His Word. She took to heart all that God had done for her people in the past and accepted that He alone could change her circumstances. To whom do you turn for solutions?

Lord, You alone can lift me from the depths of despair and set me on high places.

Listen, My Children

Your land is desolate, your cities are burned with fire,
Your fields—strangers are devouring them in your
presence; It is desolation, as overthrown by strangers. . .
Unless the Lord of hosts Had left us a few survivors,
We would be like Sodom, we would be like Gomorrah.
Hear the word of the LORD, You rulers of Sodom;
Give ear to the instruction of our God,
You people of Gomorrah.
ISAIAH 1:7, 9–10

"Listen, my children, and you shall hear of the midnight ride of Paul Revere. . ." So begins the poem "Paul Revere's Ride" by Henry Wadsworth Longfellow, required reading for many during our school days. But Paul Revere was only one of three messengers who were sent to warn the people that the British were coming.

The prophet Isaiah was also sent to warn the people of impending disaster. Here he uses an example from the past, that of Sodom and Gomorrah, to point to their own imminent doom if they fail to listen. "Hear the word of the Lord," he reminds them. These were the cities God destroyed because Abraham couldn't even find ten men there who remained obedient to God. Therefore, He rained down fire and brimstone upon them (Genesis 19:24). Before this annihilation took place, God sent His angel to warn the people. But they refused to obey.

Israel's besetting sin was idolatry, and no matter how many prophets God sent, "everyone did what was right in his own eyes" (Judges 21:25).

Lord, thank You for sending Your messengers to minister to my heart. Through them the light of Your truth finally dawned in my heart. Thank You for Your peace.

ℋIS ℒIGHT ᴅISPELS ᴅARKNESS

And Jesus cried out and said, "He who believes in
Me, does not believe in Me, but in Him who sent Me.
He who sees Me sees the One who sent me. I have come
as Light into the world, that everyone who believes in
Me may not remain in darkness."
JOHN 12:44–46

Several years ago when I worked for a countercult ministry, our group hosted a debate between one of our staff theologians and a cult leader who denied the existence of the Trinity. Although I'd read many of this man's ideas on paper, nothing prepared me for the depth of spiritual darkness he displayed that evening. But the saddest moment was peering into the spiritually dead eyes of his followers who sat only a few feet away from me.

How people can read the Word of God and reach such faulty conclusions mystifies me. If you have a question about one verse of Scripture, first, you need to pray that God's Spirit will provide enlightenment. Then, get a good study Bible that has cross-referencing indexed on each page along with the text.

Next, invest in or borrow from your church library a theological text that deals with the Bible book you are studying. Ask your pastor or minister for his personal recommendations. With such a guide at hand, God's Word becomes clearer and your faith is sure to deepen.

Your truth is readily available, Lord. Therefore, I know with certainty that I will one day see You face-to-face. Deepen my faith so that I might penetrate the spiritual darkness around me.

LEARNING TO HEAR GOD'S VOICE

The LORD called Samuel; and he said, "Here I am."
1 SAMUEL 3:4

A sleepy and startled young Samuel heard the voice calling him. Thinking it was Eli, Samuel ran to him. But Eli said, "'I did not call, lie down again.'" Being an obedient lad, Samuel again rested. But the Lord called to him again. And the whole scenario repeated again. Dismissing him, Eli told him to rest.

When this happened for the third time, Eli finally figured out that God had called to Samuel. Eli tells Samuel, "'Go lie down, and it shall be if He calls you, that you shall say, "Speak, Lord, for Thy servant is listening"'" (1 Samuel 3:9). Sure enough, the Lord did speak again. And this time Samuel responded as Eli had instructed. The Lord proceeded to say to Samuel, "'Behold, I am about to do a thing in Israel at which both ears of everyone who hears it will tingle. In that day I will carry out against Eli all that I have spoken concerning his house, from beginning to end. For I have told him that I am about to judge his house forever for the iniquity which he knew, because his sons brought a curse on themselves and he did not rebuke them'" (1 Samuel 3:11–13).

Of course this rattled Samuel's sense of well-being. Samuel wanted to keep this information from Eli, but good old Eli had already surmised that if God were ready to talk to Samuel instead of him, then He must be ready to act in judgment. So Eli asked for the truth and Samuel related the message as God presented it.

Lord, keep me close to You, that I may always hear You.

130

The Lord Provides a Sign

But Ahaz said, "I will not ask, nor will I test the Lord!"
Then he said, "Listen now, O house of David!
Is it too slight a thing for you to try the patience of
men, that you will try the patience of my God as well?
Therefore the Lord Himself will give you a sign:
Behold, a virgin will be with child and bear a son,
and she will call His name Immanuel."
Isaiah 7:12–14

In the days of Ahaz, king of Judah, two other kings went up to Jerusalem to wage war but were unable to conquer it. Their foiled efforts did not prevent King Ahaz from feeling apprehension bordering on terror.

At this point, the Lord spoke to Isaiah, saying, "Go out now to meet Ahaz. . .and say to him, 'Take care, and be calm, have no fear and do not be faint-hearted. . .on account of the fierce anger of Rezin and Aram, and the son of Remaliah. Because Aram, with Ephraim and the son of Remaliah, has planned evil against you. . .It shall not stand nor shall it come to pass" (Isaiah 7:3–5, 7).

The Lord then foretold the fact that within sixty-five years Ephraim would be shattered and no longer even a people. However, this word from the Lord wasn't sufficient proof for King Ahaz. Therefore, God said that He would provide a sign. This prediction of Christ's conception was delivered over seven hundred years before He was actually born (the fulfillment is recorded in Matthew 1:23). In announcing to Joseph that Mary was with child by the power of God's Spirit, the angel used these exact words from Isaiah.

Lord, what You have said always comes to pass. While I may entertain thoughts about being "in charge," You're out there making things happen!

Jesus' Last Passover

*During supper, the devil having already put into the
heart of Judas Iscariot, the son of Simon, to betray Him,
Jesus, knowing that the Father had given all things into
His hands, and that He had come forth from God,
and was going back to God, got up from supper, and
laid aside His garments; and taking a towel, He girded
Himself. Then He poured water into the basin,
and began to wash the disciples' feet, and to wipe
them with the towel with which He was girded.*

JOHN 13:2–5

In this one paragraph we are given reams of information about the last supper Jesus shared with His disciples. How difficult it must have been for Christ to say good-bye to them, knowing they still didn't fully comprehend His impending death! So Jesus set about to love them. By His example, He wanted to show them that they were called likewise to be servants.

Christ removed His outer garment and then placed the garb of a servant, a towel, about His waist. Then He began washing the dust from the disciples' feet. Usually a servant would administer this kindness to those who came in for the banquet supper. But the God who had created them desired that His followers know the depth of His humility. His gesture made them uncomfortable. When Peter balked as the Lord stooped to wash his feet, Jesus said, "'Do you not know what I have done to you? You call Me Teacher and Lord; and you are right, for so I am. If I then, the Lord and the Teacher, washed your feet, you also ought to wash one another's feet'" (John 13:12–14).

Lord, help me to cultivate the heart of a true servant.

Jesus, the True Vine

"I am the true vine, and My Father is the vinedresser.
Every branch in Me that does not bear fruit, He takes
away; and every branch that bears fruit, He prunes
it, that it may bear more fruit. You are already clean
because of the word which I have spoken to you.
Abide in Me, and I in you. As the branch cannot bear
fruit of itself, unless it abides in the vine, so neither can
you, unless you abide in Me. I am the vine, you are the
branches; he who abides in Me, and I in him, he bears
much fruit; for apart from Me you can do nothing."
John 15:1–5

Christ used word pictures to clarify concepts to His followers. And this parable about the vine and the branches was extremely familiar to them.

Consider Isaiah 5:1–4: "Let me sing now for my well-beloved a song of my beloved concerning His vineyard. My well-beloved had a vineyard on a fertile hill. He dug it all around, removed its stones, and planted it with the choicest vine. And He built a tower in the middle of it, and hewed out a wine vat in it; then He expected it to produce good grapes, but it produced only worthless ones. 'And now, O inhabitants of Jerusalem and men of Judah, judge between Me and My vineyard. What more was there to do for My vineyard that I have not done in it?'" No matter how faithful God was, Israel was still disobedient.

This same offer to abide in the vine is extended to all who hear the Gospel message. Have you responded? And how diligently are you abiding?

Lord, help me to abide in You.

A New Name for Israel

For Zion's sake I will not keep silent, And for Jerusalem's sake I will not keep quiet, Until her righteousness goes forth like brightness, And her salvation like a torch that is burning. The nations will see your righteousness, And all kings your glory, And you will be called by a new name, which the mouth of the LORD will designate.

ISAIAH 62:1–2

Whenever God sets about to perform a work of regeneration He also provides a new name. For instance, Abraham was known simply as Abram prior to God's promise that he would be the father of a great nation (Genesis 17:1, 5–6).

Similarly, God changed Jacob's name to Israel, and he became the father of the twelve tribes of Israel (Genesis 32:28).

Then there are the passages we've studied concerning the names God picked out for people before they were even born. Zechariah was told to name his son John. Mary and Joseph were told that our Savior's name was to be Jesus Christ.

In today's Scripture the Lord is addressing His people's repeated disobedience which has caused Israel's name to became synonymous with "Forsaken" and "Desolate" (Isaiah 62:4). However, they will one day become the Redeemed of the Lord, God's Holy People. Then they will be called, "Sought out, a city not forsaken" (Isaiah 62:12).

Lord, my name remains the same, but my heart is forever changed by Your love.

Saul, Israel's King

Now there was a man of Benjamin whose name was
Kish the son of Abiel, the son of Zertror, the son of
Becorath, the son of Aphiah, the son of a Benjamite,
a mighty man of valor. He had a son whose name was
Saul, a choice and handsome man, and there was not a
more handsome person than he among the sons of Israel;
from his shoulders and up he was taller
than any of the people.
1 Samuel 9:1–2

Isn't that exactly what our society looks for in the way of leaders? One who is tall and handsome and reeks of success! But outward appearance means nothing if that person isn't fully committed to God.

Saul had been on a mission. It seems that his father's donkeys had gotten loose. As Saul and his servant went from place to place attempting to track them down, they reached the land of Zuph and frustrated, decided to return home. But this servant knew that there was a man of God in the town and he encouraged Saul to speak to the man.

Of course, God had already prepared Samuel's heart: "'About this time tomorrow I will send you a man from the land of Benjamin, and you shall anoint him to be prince over My people Israel, and he shall deliver My people from the hand of the Philistines. For I have regarded My people, because their cry has come to Me'" (1 Samuel 9:16).

God chose Saul to be Israel's king so that this nation might eventually learn their need for spiritual discernment.

Lord, when I seek a direction You have neither sanctioned nor initiated, please reveal the truth to me, that I might not have to learn life's lessons the hard way.

CALLED TO CONQUER?

*"About this time tomorrow I will send you a man from
the land of Benjamin, and you shall anoint him to be
prince over my people Israel; and he shall deliver
My people from the hand of the Philistines."*
1 SAMUEL 9:16

Despite Israel's repeated disobedience, God continued to love Israel and respond to the people's requests.
And although the Israelites stubbornly refused to
allow Him to rule over them as King, they did desire
an earthly king.

When Saul met with Samuel, Samuel, acting
as mediator between God and man, related that the
donkeys Saul had been seeking were now found.
Samuel confirmed that this special leadership call was
from the Lord. "Then Samuel took the flask of oil,
poured it on his head, kissed him and said, 'Has not
the Lord anointed you a ruler over His inheritance?'"
(1 Samuel 10:1)

God had already prepared a celebration for Saul,
befitting his royal status. And the Lord instructed him
to go to the oak of Tabor, a sacred spot where Jacob
had built an altar when God had revealed Himself to
him (Genesis 35:6, 7; 1 Samuel 10:3).

Notice that Saul's call was to conquer the
Philistines. His anointing had been done secretly,
but now Samuel assembled all Israel and "the tribe of
Benjamin was taken by lot" (1 Samuel 10:20). When
Saul failed to appear ". . .they inquired further of the
Lord. . .So the Lord said, 'Behold, he is hiding himself
by the baggage'" (1 Samuel 10:22).

*Lord, help me trust in Your strength to instill, infuse,
and instruct so that I serve You obediently.*

Jeremiah's Revival

Now the word of the Lord came to me saying,
"Before I formed you in the womb I knew you,
And before you were born I consecrated you; I have
appointed you a prophet to the nations."
Jeremiah 1:4–5

Knowing that he was called, chosen, and consecrated should have given Jeremiah a great deal of confidence. However, like any true prophet, he felt consumed because of his own inadequacies. "Then I said, 'Alas, Lord God! Behold, I do not know how to speak, Because I am a youth'" (Jeremiah 1:6).

"But the Lord said to me, 'Do not say, "I am a youth," Because everywhere I send you, you shall go, And all that I command you, you shall speak. Do not be afraid of them, For I am with you to deliver you,' declares the Lord. Then the Lord stretched out His hand and touched my mouth, and the Lord said to me, 'Behold, I have put My words in your mouth'" (Jeremiah 1:7–9). And Jeremiah proceeded forward, fulfilling his mission.

Jeremiah prophesied prior to and during Babylon's three sieges of Judah. Revival came when the Word of the Lord was found in the house of God as Josiah, the last king of Judah, called the people to repentance. However, following this great time of worship, Israel's disobedience once again set in, bringing upon them yet again God's heavy hand of judgment. And Jeremiah the prophet wept.

Lord, I pray for answers to the dilemmas that plague
our society. Not knowing whom You have called for
special service, let me respect and revere each life with
hope, anticipation, and gratitude.

Jeremiah's Vision

"For, behold, I am calling all the families of the kingdoms of the north," declares the LORD; *"and they will come, and they will set each one his throne at the entrance of the gates of Jerusalem, and against all its walls round about, and against all the cities of Judah. I will pronounce My judgments on them concerning all their wickedness, whereby they have forsaken Me and have offered sacrifices to other gods, and worshiped the works of their own hands."*

JEREMIAH 1:15–16

Israel's roller-coaster ride of faithfulness had once again begun its downward plunge. Despite all God's warnings, the people failed to responded to Him unless they were in dire pain. Therefore, the Lord encourages Jeremiah by saying, "'Now, gird up your loins, and arise, and speak to them all which I command you. Do not be dismayed before them, lest I dismay you before them. . .And they will fight against you, but they will not overcome you, for I am with you to deliver you'" (Jeremiah 1:17, 19).

We humans are resilient, able to withstand almost any hardship as long as we know we're not abandoned. God always provides a way through, for Israel and for us. His instructions to Israel read almost like a love letter: "'I remember concerning you the devotion of your youth, the love of your betrothals, your following after Me in the wilderness, through a land not sown. Israel was holy to the Lord, the first of His harvest. . .'" (Jeremiah 2:2–3).

Lord, if I'm about to head off in the wrong direction, please call me back. I'll never be truly happy apart from You.

QUESTION THE WITNESSES

The high priest then questioned Jesus about His disciples, and about His teaching. Jesus answered him, "I have spoken openly to the world; I always taught in synagogues, and in the temple, where all the Jews come together; and I spoke nothing in secret. Why do you question Me? Question those who have heard what I spoke to them; they know what I said."
JOHN 18:19–21

In our courts of law the jury is instructed to listen carefully and then weigh the testimony to make a proper judgment. Christ calls the high priest to do the same.

How do we respond to the truth of Christ's testimony? How we treat His messengers is, in effect, a measure of our acceptance of Him.

Jesus Christ didn't come for a few souls; He presented the Gospel message openly for all to hear. Teaching in the Jewish temple, which was frequented not only by those who sought knowledge but also those in search of an explanation of the truth, Jesus provided both.

As we go out into a world that is hostile to the Gospel message, there are those who listen to our testimony and then draw near to its refreshing waters. Others sit on the river banks, vowing that nothing will force them to make a life change. And then there are those who deny the metamorphosis has even taken place. Their hearts are closed to receive the truth.

Lord, break down my walls of stubbornness that prevent me from hearing, seeing, and rallying to Your message.

ᗞAVID ᏚLINGS A ᏚTONE

"For who is this uncircumcised Philistine, that he should taunt the armies of the living God?"
1 SAMUEL 17:26

David, while still a youth, came up against a giant of a man. "Then a champion came out from the armies of the Philistines named Goliath, from Gath, whose height was six cubits and a span" (1 Samuel 17:4).

This superhuman specimen had the audacity to taunt Israel's God. And David refused to allow this attitude to stand unchallenged.

Then David said to the Philistine, "'You come to me with a sword, a spear, and a javelin, but I come to you in the name of the Lord of hosts, the God of the armies of Israel, whom you have taunted. This day the Lord will deliver you up into my hands, and I will strike you down and remove your head from you. And I will give the dead bodies of the army of the Philistines this day to the birds of the sky and the wild beasts of the earth, that all the earth may know that there is a God in Israel'" (1 Samuel 17:45–46).

"And David put his hand into his bag and took from it a stone and slung it, and struck the Philistine on his forehead. And the stone sank into his forehead, so that he fell on his face to the ground" (1 Samuel 17:49).

David's victory came by the power of the Lord, not by man's might. Lord, remind me of this when I face my own "giants."

A Promise of Unity

"In those days. . .declares the Lord, "they shall say no more, 'The ark of the covenant of the LORD.' And it will not come to mind, nor will they remember it, nor will they miss it, nor will it be made again. At that time they will call Jerusalem 'The Throne of the LORD,' and all the nations will be gathered to it, to Jerusalem, for the name of the Lord; nor shall they walk any more after the stubbornness of their evil heart. In those days the house of Judah will walk with the house of Israel, and they will come together from the land of the north to the land that I gave your fathers as an inheritance."

JEREMIAH 3:16–18

Jeremiah delivered hope to the people of Israel during Judah's three-stage siege.

This three-pronged prophecy also related God's future plans for Israel. First, the ark of the covenant would be gone, not remembered, and never made again. Next, Jerusalem would be called "The Throne of the Lord," where all nations would be gathered in the name of the Lord. Finally, the houses of Judah and Israel, separated due to the Babylonian captivity, would once again be united.

In the year 586 BC, Solomon's temple was utterly destroyed. At the same time, the ark of the covenant was lost. God's glory had departed from Israel. For this reason, God's confirmation that Jerusalem would once again become the center for worship became critically important. During King Herod's reign the temple was rebuilt, fulfilling part of this prophecy. And when Jesus Christ came, it had once again become the center of worship.

True peace will reign in Israel when Christ returns again to earth (Matthew 24:29–39). Lord, help me wait!

141

CROWN OF MOCKERY

Pilate then took Jesus and scourged Him.
And the soldiers twisted together a crown of thorns and
put it on His head, and arrayed Him in a purple robe;
and they began to come up to Him, and say, "Hail,
King of the Jews!" and to give Him slaps in the face.
JOHN 19:1–3

They pretended to shower Him with all the outward trappings of royalty. But this homage was one of cruel mockery. The thorns were razor-sharp briars about an inch and a half long. We can only imagine the taunting voices of these men, triumphant glances spreading across their faces as they pressed this crown into Christ's head until blood ran down His face.

Then the men handed Him "a reed in His right hand; and they kneeled down before Him and mocked Him saying, 'Hail, King of the Jews!' And they spat on Him, and took the reed and began to beat Him on the head. And after they had mocked Him, they took His robe off and put His garments on Him, and led Him away to crucify Him" (Matthew 27: 29–31). This action fulfilled the prophetic Psalm 22:18: "They divide my garments among them, and for my clothing they cast lots."

"He was despised and forsaken of men, A man of sorrows, and acquainted with grief; And like one from whom men hide their face, He was despised, and we did not esteem Him" (Isaiah 53:3).

Lord, in my behalf You withstood extreme torture. Am I adding new but invisible wounds each time I refuse to crown You King of my own life?

JONATHAN, FAITHFUL TO THE END

Now the Philistines were fighting against Israel,
and the men of Israel fled from before the Philistines and
fell slain on Mount Gilboa. The Philistines overtook Saul
and his sons; and the Philistines killed Jonathan and
Abinadab and Malachi-shua the sons of Saul.
1 SAMUEL 31:1–2

Who has faithfully stood beside you through life's triumphs and tragedies? For David this person was Jonathan.

Jonathan walked a tightrope, remaining faithful to God, to Saul, his father, and to David. Considering Saul's obsession with killing David, this task took on monstrous proportions.

Their friendship began shortly after David killed the giant Goliath. Jonathan even gave David his "armor, including his sword and bow and belt" (1 Samuel 18:4). And how quickly David would need these weapons! David's accomplishments in battle became the stuff of legend and song, and this, of course, enraged Saul.

From then on Jonathan's time was spent trying to help David keep one step ahead of Saul. "So Jonathan told David saying, 'Saul my father is seeking to put you to death. Now therefore, please be on guard in the morning, and stay in a secret place and hide yourself. And I will go out and stand beside my father in the field where you are, and I will speak with my father about you; if I find out anything, then I shall tell you'" (1 Samuel 19:2–3).

Father, help me to be a faithful, loving, and unforgettable friend.

The First to View the Resurrection

Mary Magdalene came early to the tomb, while it was
still dark, and saw the stone already taken away from
the tomb. So she ran and came to Simon Peter, and to
the other disciple whom Jesus loved, and said to them,
"They have taken away the Lord out of the tomb,
and we do not know where they have laid Him."
John 20:1–2

If only the disciples had understood the Scriptures concerning Christ's resurrection.

Peter and John ran to the tomb, viewed the linen wrappings, and then left again (John 20:8–10). They left too soon, missing the miracle. "But Mary was standing outside the tomb weeping; and so, as she wept, she stooped and looked into the tomb; and she beheld two angels in white sitting, one at the head, and one at the feet, where the body of Jesus had been lying. And they said to her, 'Woman, why are you weeping?' She said to them, 'Because they have taken away my Lord, and I do not know where they have laid Him.' When she had said this, she turned around, and beheld Jesus standing there, and did not know that it was Jesus" (John 20:11–14).

Mary supposed that Christ was a gardener. Therefore, she said to him, "'Sir, if you have carried Him away, tell me where you have laid Him, and I will take Him away'" (John 20:15).

But then He said, "'Mary!'" And the sound of His voice calmed her frantic fears, dried her tears, and warmed her heart.

Lord, many times I miss the miracle You have already
prepared. Open my eyes!

David Learns of Saul's Death

"The people have fled from the battle, and also many of the people have fallen and are dead; and Saul and Jonathan his son are dead also."

2 Samuel 1:4

A young Amalekite man had related to David that Saul and Jonathan were dead. Then he confessed that Saul had been impaled on his own sword and begged him to kill him. After complying with this request, the Amalekite then removed the crown from Saul's head and the bracelet that was on his arm and brought these royal ornaments to David.

First David led Israel in a time of mourning for Saul. "Then David took hold of his clothes and tore them, and so also did all the men who were with him. And they mourned and wept and fasted until evening" (2 Samuel 1:11–12).

Following this expression of sorrow came a time of retribution. "Then David said to him, 'How is it you were not afraid to stretch out your hand to destroy the Lord's anointed?' And David called one of the young men and said, 'Go, cut him down.' So he struck him and he died" (2 Samuel 1:14–15).

David poured forth his personal anguish by writing a song for Saul and Jonathan. One verse reads, "'Saul and Jonathan, beloved and pleasant in their life, and in their death they were not parted; they were swifter than eagles, they were stronger than lions'" (2 Samuel 1:23).

Lord, what an example David was, as he refused to gloat over Saul's death. David turned to You and requested guidance, and You gave him a fresh call to leadership. I rejoice!

145

EZEKIEL'S CALL

While I was by the river Chebar among the exiles,
the heavens were opened and I saw visions of God.
(On the fifth of the month in the fifth year of
King Jehoiachin's exile, the word of the LORD came
expressly to Ezekiel the priest, son of Buzi, in the
land of the Chaldeans by the river Chebar; and
there the hand of the LORD came upon him.)
EZEKIEL 1:1–3

Sometimes God's plans are so different from what we expect to be doing with our lives that it's really astonishing.

Although he was only eighteen years old when some of the nobles and princes were captured by King Nebuchadnezzar and taken from Judah to Babylon, Ezekiel had already been groomed for the priesthood.

Ezekiel's life plan became forever altered ten years later, in 597 BC, when he was among those taken in Nebuchadnezzar's second siege against Jerusalem. Never again would he view the temple where he had hoped to serve God. However, when he was thirty years old the Lord gave him a vision of a new temple and another Jerusalem. His call was to prophesy concerning Judah and Jerusalem, Israel's coming restoration, and the temple.

Ezekiel's visions parallel those of John recorded in the Book of Revelation. These dreams show that no matter how bleak Israel's present situation might be, their future would be bright.

Lord, despite my own problems and challenges I can keep going forward as long as You show me a vision of hope. As I read the prophecies of Ezekiel, fill me with expectation!

Always a Remnant

"So as I live," declares the Lord GOD, "surely, because you have defiled My sanctuary with all your detestable idols and with all your abominations, therefore I will also withdraw, and My eye shall have no pity and I will not spare."

EZEKIEL 5:11

Only the nation of Israel has managed to survive being scattered all over the globe and then come back to become a world power. How is this possible? God always preserves a remnant of His people. And it will be so until the end of time on this earth. "'One third of you will die by plague or be consumed by famine among you, one third will fall by the sword around you, and one third I will scatter to every wind, and I will unsheathe a sword behind them'" (Ezekiel 5:12).

God is executing judgment on them because they abandoned their worship of the true God, choosing instead to adopt the ways of the pagan nations which surrounded them.

But how do we know this cycle will continue until the end of time? Four angels stand ready to execute God's judgment on the whole world. And they are restrained from action until "one hundred and forty-four thousand were sealed from every tribe of the sons of Israel" (Revelation 7:4). Twelve thousand from each of the tribes of Israel will be marked by God's own hand.

Many terrible plagues and judgments will take place upon the earth. However, God will bring this remnant of Israel safely through it all.

Father, I rejoice in Your Word: "'And then He will send forth the angels, and will gather together His elect. . .from the farthest end of the earth, to the farthest end of heaven'" (Mark 13:27).

147

A False Peace

"So My hand will be against the prophets who see false visions and utter lying divinations. They will have no place in the council of My people, nor will they be written down in the register of the house of Israel, nor will they enter the land of Israel, that you may know that I am the Lord God. It is definitely because they have misled My people by saying, 'Peace!' when there is no peace."
EZEKIEL 13:9–10

People today get sick of hearing modern doomsday forecasters who shout, "Turn or burn." Those living in Ezekiel's day reacted the same way. They preferred to listen to those who preached a message of peace rather than the need for repentance.

I'll never forget one Thanksgiving Day prayer. The peace accord between Israel and Egypt had just been signed and so at the dinner table one of our relatives proclaimed that peace now reigned upon the earth. Although I knew he was sincere, I couldn't help but stare in amazement. Didn't he realize there would never be true peace until the Prince of Peace reigned in people's hearts? Of course, true to form, unrest began again.

Just as Ezekiel could not remain complacent in the midst of false peacegivers, those of our own day who know the truth are obligated to bring the message of repentance and salvation to others. How else will they hear and respond?

Lord, help me to share Your truth or assist others to do so, even in the midst of an apathetic and, yes, hostile world.

$\mathscr{D}$AVID'S $\mathscr{R}$OCK, $\mathscr{F}$ORTRESS, AND $\mathscr{D}$ELIVERER

"The Lord is my rock and my fortress and my deliverer;
My God, my rock, in whom I take refuge; My shield and
the horn of my salvation, my stronghold and my refuge;
My savior, Thou dost save me from violence."

2 SAMUEL 22:2–3

David's understanding of his Lord, using this concept of refuge, is a picture of the peace, comfort, and security we seek for our lives.

Although David spoke of the Rocks of the Wild Goats (1 Samuel 24:2), where he and his men hid from Saul, this analogy was also used to describe the believer's destination of spiritual serenity in the Rock, who is Christ.

David depended on the Lord as his Rock of faith. "Let the words of my mouth and the meditation of my heart Be acceptable in Your sight, O Lord, my rock and my Redeemer" (Psalm 19:14).

However, to those who choose not to believe, Christ becomes only a stumbling block. "But Israel, pursuing a law of righteousness, did not arrive at that law. Why? Because they did not pursue it by faith, but as though it were by works. They stumbled over the stumbling stone, just as it is written, 'Behold, I lay in Zion a stone of stumbling and a rock of offense, And he who belives in Him will not be disappointed'" (Romans 9:30–33).

I praise You only, Jesus, my Rock of Faith and Redeemer.

ℬAPTISM OF ℛEPENTANCE

"Repent, and let each of you be baptized in the name of
Jesus Christ for the forgiveness of your sins;
and you will receive the gift of the Holy Spirit."
ACTS 2:38

Many of us were christened or baptized as infants. While this is a beautiful as well as meaningful service, such a rite does not cleanse a person from sin.

Jesus said, "'The time is fulfilled, and the kingdom of God is at hand; repent and believe in the gospel'" (Mark 1:15). There's no getting around His meaning here. One first has to come face-to-face with her need for salvation before she can receive this great gift. How can an infant make such a choice?

Belief comes in response to presentation of the Word: "Then He opened their minds to understand the Scriptures, and He said to them, 'Thus it is written, that the Christ should suffer and rise again from the dead the third day; and that repentance for forgiveness of sins should be proclaimed in His name to all the nations, beginning from Jerusalem'" (Luke 24:45–47).

Also, it's critical to note that the Holy Spirit is given at the moment of repentance (Acts 2:38). In the Gospel of Mark, quoted above, we know for certain that God's time-table for obtaining salvation has begun.

Lord, I thank You that those who lived before Jesus came to earth were given the same gospel message through the prophets. I thank You that You have always provided a way to salvation.

A Dance in the Fiery Furnace

Then the herald loudly proclaimed: ". . .O peoples,
nations and men of every language, that you are
to fall down and worship the golden image that
Nebuchadnezzar the king has set up."
DANIEL 3:4–5

Although King Nebuchadnezzar had witnessed God's power and even acknowledged it, he had now retreated to unbelief.

In fact, the king had now slipped into total egotism, making an image of gold that represented himself and then demanding worship from the people. The king's advisors used this proclamation to entrap Daniel's friends, who refused to bow down to any king but the Lord. Therefore, Shadrach, Meshach, and Abednego were bound and then thrown into a fiery furnace and it was heated "seven times more than it was usually" (Daniel 3:19–20).

But when the king looked into the furnace he saw a fourth person in the midst of the fire. "'Look! I see four men loosed and walking about in the midst of the fire without harm, and the appearance of the fourth is like a son of the gods!'" (Daniel 3:25) So the king ordered them out again.

Jesus was with Daniel's friends in the fire. "'When you walk through the fire, you will not be scorched, nor will the flame burn you. For I am the Lord your God, the Holy One of Israel, your Savior'" (Isaiah 43:2–3).

Lord, be my faithful God, just as You were to Daniel's
friends. Keep me from harm as I walk through the fires
in my own life.

A True Mother's Love

"Now, O LORD my God, You have made Your servant
king in place of my father David, yet I am but a little
child; I do not know how to go out or come in.
Your servant is in the midst of Your people which You
have chosen, a great people who cannot be numbered or
counted. So give Your servant an understanding heart
to judge Your people to discern between good and evil.
For who is able to judge this great people of Yours?"
1 KINGS 3:7–9

Shortly after King Solomon had asked the Lord for wisdom, two harlots brought their case before him. Each woman stated that one particular infant belonged to her. Obviously one of them was lying. You see, one woman's child had died shortly after his birth and she had taken the other woman's live baby, laying her dead son in the other mother's arms.

As they stood arguing and shouting, Solomon said, "'Get me a sword.' So they brought a sword before the king. And the king said, 'Divide the living child in two, and give half to the one and half to the other'" (1 Kings 3:24–25). Solomon knew that the child's true mother would come to the baby's defense.

Within minutes the issue was resolved and the real mother held her child again. "When all Israel heard of the judgment which the king had handed down, they feared the king; for they saw that the wisdom of God was in him to administer justice" (1 Kings 3:28).

Lord, how I pray that such wisdom would be given to lawmakers. I also need Your guidance for my family. Help me remember to turn to You in my dilemmas.

Saul and Stephen

*They went on stoning Stephen as he called upon the
Lord and said, "Lord Jesus, receive my spirit!"
Then falling on his knees, he cried out with a loud voice,
"Lord, do not hold this sin against them!" Having said
this, he fell asleep. Saul was in hearty agreement with
putting him to death. And on that day a great
persecution arose against the church in Jerusalem.*
Acts 7:59–60; 8:1

Have you ever committed an action so despicable
that you can't imagine God could ever forgive you?
Saul—who would soon be acclaimed as the fearless
apostle Paul—had been persuaded by his own pious
intentions to stamp out the Gospel's heresy. After the
stoning of Stephen, Saul entered home after home
and dragged Christians off to prison.

And then the powerful hand of the Lord God
intervened.

"Suddenly a light from heaven flashed around
him; and he fell to the ground, and heard a voice saying to him, 'Saul, Saul, why are you persecuting Me?'
And he said, 'Who are You, Lord?' And He said, 'I am
Jesus whom you are persecuting, but rise, and enter
the city, and it shall be told you what you must do'"
(Acts 9:3–6).

Blinded for three days by God's incredible power,
Saul had to be led into the city of Damascus. There,
a disciple named Ananias, to whom God gave a message, would intervene.

Thank You, God, for changing Saul into Paul!

All the King's Horses

*Solomon amassed chariots and horsemen. He had
1, 400 chariots, and 12,000 horsemen, and he stationed them in the chariot cities and with the king at
Jerusalem. . .Solomon's horses were imported from
Egypt and from Kue; the king's traders procured them
from Kue for a price. They imported chariots from
Egypt for 600 shekels of silver apiece, and horses for
150 apiece, and by the same means they exported them
to all the kings of the Hittites and the kings of Aram.*
2 CHRONICLES 1:14, 16–17

Solomon's horses were the finest that money could
buy. But they weren't just for pleasure. These valiant
steeds helped defend his kingdom and also provided
revenue as they were sold or loaned to other kings.

Solomon's horses were stationed in strategic cities, ready to guard and protect the kingdom. And in
1 Kings 4:26 we see that "Solomon had 40,000 stalls
of horses for his chariots." He also had deputies who
"brought barley and straw for the horses and swift
steeds to the place where it should be, each according
to his charge" (1 Kings 4:28).

Long before Israel even had a king, the Lord had
established certain standards for this monarch. He
was not to multiply horses for himself, nor cause the
people to return to Egypt to get horses (Deuteronomy
17:14–16). God didn't want the king's heart to turn
away from following Him.

*Had Solomon followed God's commands, his kingdom
would have been assured of survival. Lord, help me to
remain faithful.*

ANTICHRIST, THE RULER TO COME

"In his place a despicable person will arise, on whom the honor of kingship has not been conferred, but he will come in a time of tranquility and seize the kingdom by intrigue. The overflowing forces will be flooded away before him and shattered, and also the prince of the covenant. And after an alliance is made with him he will practice deception, and he will go up and gain power with a small force of people. In a time of tranquility he will enter the richest parts of the realm, and he will accomplish what his fathers never did, nor his ancestors; he will distribute plunder, booty, and possessions among them, and he will devise his schemes against strongholds, but only for a time."

DANIEL 11:21–24

The antichrist is a real person who will one day deviously slither onto the scene right on cue. He will appear indispensable at a time of worldwide, unsolvable chaos. His allies will be the foes of God.

His deception will be so great that people will fail to see his face of evil until "the abomination of desolation" takes place (Matthew 24:15). Three and one-half years after he comes on the scene, the antichrist will enter the rebuilt temple in Jerusalem, declare himself god, and demand worship and allegiance from the world. Jesus Himself warned the Jews about this diabolical person, telling them that when they saw him to "'let those who are in Judea flee to the mountains'" (Mark 13:14).

Lord, compel me with new urgency to study Your powerful Word, that I might bring it to others.

Michael Stands Guard

*"Now at that time Michael, the great prince who
stands guard over the sons of your people, will arise.
And there will be a time of distress such as never
occurred since there was a nation until that time;
and at that time your people, everyone who is
found written in the book, will be rescued."*
Daniel 12:1

The prophet Daniel spoke of the archangel Michael because he wanted Israel to be aware that God had already given them a great prince who stands guard over them. Those whose names are written in the book will be spared. God writes the names in His book. It's called the Lamb's book of life. "And the city has no need of the sun or of the moon to shine upon it, for the glory of God has illumined it, and its lamp is the Lamb. . .and nothing unclean and no one who practices abomination and lying, shall ever come into it, but only those whose names are written in the Lamb's book of life" (Revelation 21:23, 27). When we come to believe in the Lamb, Jesus Christ, we are cleansed from our sins.

It is these, whose names are written in the book, who will be rescued from destruction: "'These are the ones who come out of the great tribulation, and they have washed their robes and made them white in the blood of the Lamb. For this reason, they are before the throne of God; and they serve Him day and night in His temple; and He who sits on the throne shall spread His tabernacle over them'" (Revelation 7:14–15).

*Lamb of God, who takes away sin, I want to know my
name is written in Your book!*

But What about the Jews?

*For if Abraham was justified by works, he has something
to boast about, but not before God. For what does the
Scripture say? "Abraham believed God,
and it was credited to Him as righteousness."*

Romans 4:2–3

Our work ethic is as old as the Garden of Eden.
Because of sin Adam's free ride was over and he would
now have to earn a living. But God said, "'Because you
have listened to the voice of your wife, and have eaten
from the tree about which I commanded you, saying, "You shall not eat from it"; Cursed is the ground
because of you; In toil you shall eat of it all the days of
your life'" (Genesis 3:17).

Somehow men and women have transferred
this attitude about working for things to salvation.
However, salvation is not based on our "goodness" but
rather on Christ's. For no matter how diligently we try
to keep those Ten Commandments, we're going to fail.

God made Abraham, the one the Jews claim as
their father, a promise and he believed God.

His belief wasn't merely an intellectual assent.
The "Supreme God of the Universe," who made absolutely everything that Abraham now saw in his world,
had deigned not only to speak to him, but He promised him an heir. The reason that Abraham could
place his trust in God was because God kept His
promises. No matter how impossible the situation
looks, God always comes through.

*I thank You that I worship a God whose Word can be
trusted. I know Jesus will always be there for me.*

GOMER, A PICTURE OF ISRAEL

*The LORD said to Hosea, "Go, take to yourself a wife
of harlotry, and have children of harlotry; for the
land commits flagrant harlotry, forsaking the Lord."
So he went and took Gomer the daughter of Diblaim,
and she conceived and bore him a son.*
HOSEA 1:2–3

Do you have a child who has wandered away from
every good thing you tried to give him? Your heart
has broken as that child perhaps chose a lifestyle that
so contradicted your own. Now imagine God going
through this same kind of pain as an entire nation,
one He dearly loved, refused to walk with Him.

Why would God ask the prophet Hosea to enter
into an unwholesome alliance? Because He wanted
Israel to understand what it was like to observe the
one to whom they were betrothed go off and play the
harlot. When Israel entered into the covenant with
God, the people had promised fidelity to Him. But
this beloved nation had "prostituted" themselves in
worship of false gods, forsaking their true God.

The Book of Hosea reveals the brokenness of
God's own heart as He watched Israel wander away.
Now God was forced to take action against the peo-
ple He loved, in order to bring them back to Him.

*"'And I will say to those who were not My people, "You
are My people!"'"* (Hosea 2:23) *Lord, thank You for
Your unique invitation.*

Peace Despite our Trials

Therefore, having been justified by faith, we have peace with God through our Lord Jesus Christ, through whom also we have obtained our introduction by faith into this grace in which we stand; and we exult in hope of the glory of God. . . For while we were still helpless, at the right time Christ died for the ungodly.

ROMANS 5:1–2, 6

People have scoured every nook and cranny of the globe in search of peace. From yoga and transcendental meditation to new age tranquility tapes and self-empowerment courses, people will try just about anything. But do these methods work?

Of course not! Instead, each new road eventually leads to the dead ends of dissatisfaction and emptiness. "I have seen all the works which have been done under the sun, and behold, all is vanity and striving after the wind" (Ecclesiastes 1:14). The promises of peace this world has to offer are nothing more than vapors of an expensive fragrance.

Enduring tranquility cannot be found outside a relationship with Christ. So why can't we just believe it's that simple?

Maybe we're simply afraid to end the search. Before I became a Christian I can recall thinking of God as my "ace in the hole." If all else failed, I'd try religion. And when all the other inlets I traveled led to dry lake beds, I did reach out for religion. However, this too was but an attempt on my part to "be good enough for God." Human effort doesn't bring peace.

Lord, I know the only true and lasting peace comes from Jesus Christ.

An Evil Plan Backfires

*"The document which you sent to us has been translated
and read before me. A decree has been issued by me,
and a search has been made and it has been discovered
that the city has risen up against the kings in past days,
that rebellion and revolt have been perpetrated in it."*

Ezra 4:18–19

In *The Music Man*, the people of River City only become aware that there's trouble in their town when the music man, Professor Harold Hill, tells them how bad off they really are. In today's Scripture, King Artaxerxes is just about as unaware of a problem until this same kind of scenario tickles his ears.

The enemies of Judah and Benjamin worry him over the potential of lost revenue. Next, they speak of how horrific it would be to see the king dishonored. Finally, they intimate that past problems with the Israelites can be proven by obtaining the record books.

"Then as soon as the copy of King Artaxerxes' document was read before Rehum and Shimshai the scribe and their colleagues, they went in haste to Jerusalem to the Jews and stopped them by force of arms. Then the work on the house of God in Jerusalem ceased, and it was stopped until the second year of the reign of Darius king of Persia" (Ezra 4:23–24).

"But the eye of their God was on the elders of the Jews, and they did not stop them until a report should come to Darius, and then a written reply he returned concerning it" (Ezra 5:5). When the inquiry was made, it gave the Israelites a chance to expound on how the decree had gone out by Cyrus, king of Babylon, to rebuild the house of God (Ezra 5:6–13).

Lord, I read that shortly after King Darius issued a decree, work began again to finish Your temple. Your will is always done!

JOEL AND A PLAGUE OF LOCUSTS

What the gnawing locust has left, the swarming locust
has eaten. . .and what the creeping locust has left,
the stripping locust has eaten.
JOEL 1:4

Joel's words could provide a great plot line for a sci-fi thriller. The worst thing about this plague is that it seemingly came upon the people without warning and was more devastating than anything they'd ever witnessed (Joel 1:1–7). Other catastrophes would follow.

The apostle Peter explained Pentecost in light of Joel's prophecy: " 'This is what was spoken of through the prophet Joel: "And it shall be in the last days," God says, "That I will in those days pour forth of My Spirit and they shall prophesy. And I will grant wonders in the sky above, And signs on the earth beneath. . . Before the great and glorious day of the Lord shall come. And it shall be, that everyone who calls on the name of the Lord shall be saved" ' " (Acts 2:16–21).

The information contained in the book of Joel is referred to as eschatology, or a study of the end times, and parallels other passages in Scripture. When Jesus spoke to His disciples, He too quoted this prophetic passage, providing additional clarity.

Lord, I rejoice in Your Word: " 'But immediately after
the tribulation. . .the sign of the Son of Man will appear
in the sky. . .and they will see the Son of Man coming on
the clouds of the clouds of the sky with power and great
glory' " (Matthew 24:29–30).

Paul's Prayer for the Jews

*Brethren, my heart's desire and my prayer to
God for them is for their salvation.*
ROMANS 10:1

Is the deepest concern of your heart that those whom you love will share heaven with Christ? The deepest longing of Paul's soul was that the Jews might know their Messiah.

Paul longed for the Israelites, "to whom belongs the adoption as sons and the glory and the covenants and the giving of the Law and the temple service and the promises," to understand that Christ had come to save them (Romans 9:4–5).

The Jews couldn't truly be God's children until they partook of the light of truth. "For the Scripture says, 'Whoever believes in Him will not be disappointed.' For there is no distinction between Jew and Greek; for the same Lord is Lord of all, abounding in riches for all who call upon Him; for 'Whoever will call upon the name of the Lord will be saved'" (Romans 10:11–13).

Paul presents the simple process by which they can become cleansed of their sins. "But what does it say? 'The word is near you, in your mouth and in your heart'—that is, the word of faith which we are preaching, that if you confess with your mouth Jesus as Lord, and believe in your heart that God raised Him from the dead, you shall be saved; for with the heart man believes, resulting in righteousness, and with the mouth he confesses, resulting in salvation" (Romans 10:8–10).

Lord, clarify Your Word, that women may yield in faith.

$\mathcal{N}$EHEMIAH AND THE $\mathcal{W}$ALLS OF $\mathcal{J}$ERUSALEM

"The remnant there in the province who survived the captivity are in great distress and reproach, and the wall of Jerusalem is broken down and its gates are burned with fire." When I heard these words, I sat down and wept and mourned for days; and I was fasting and praying before the God of heaven.

NEHEMIAH 1:3–4

Nehemiah records the events that took place as Jerusalem's walls were repaired. Fortified walls were necessary not only to guard the perimeter of the great city, but also to demonstrate the renewed pride and unity of its citizens.

Although Nehemiah was in Susa, the Persian capital, which was 600 miles away, he couldn't forget either his beloved city or its people. So, he poured out heartfelt prayers to the Lord, seeking His wisdom for this great renovation project. And God's reply caused him to mourn, fast and weep, as the solution to Israel's problem crystallized: "'We have sinned against Thee; I and my father's house have sinned'" (Nehemiah 1:6).

Then Nehemiah requested that King Artaxerxes send him to Judah that he might rebuild the walls. And all of Nehemiah's time of fasting and prayer were answered as the king wrote letters of safe passage for him to all "the governors of the provinces beyond the River" (Nehemiah 2:7). In God's timing Nehemiah shared his plan with the remnant of Israel.

Lord, let me learn from Nehemiah's example. Let me seek Your will through prayer and study, never losing sight of Your Son.

JOEL PROPHESIES A FINAL JUDGMENT

Hasten and come, all you surrounding nations,
and gather yourselves there. Bring down, O Lord,
Your mighty ones. Let the nations be aroused and
come up to the valley of Jehoshaphat, for there I will
sit to judge all the surrounding nations.
JOEL 3:11–12

Jerusalem will be the site of the world's last and greatest battle as all the surrounding nations rage against the Holy City. However, the powerful, almighty God of the universe will intervene on Israel's behalf.

"The Lord roars from Zion and utters His voice from Jerusalem, and the heavens and the earth tremble. But the LORD is a refuge for His people and a stronghold to the sons of Israel. Then you will know that I am the LORD your God, dwelling in Zion, My holy mountain. So Jerusalem will be holy, and strangers will pass through it no more" (Joel 3:16–17).

God gave the prophet Isaiah a similar message: "For the law will go forth from Zion, and the word of the LORD from Jerusalem. And He will judge between the nations" (Isaiah 2:3–4).

When will this last and greatest battle take place? At the end of the age, when Christ comes back to conquer all those who have attempted to ravage His people and their city. "And I looked, and behold, a white cloud, and sitting on the cloud was one like a son of man, having a golden crown on His head, and a sharp sickle in His hand" (Revelation 14:14).

Lord, I don't like to consider the brutality of this final judgment. However, I know that You are fair and just and have given men and women ample time and warning to repent.

Renewing Our Minds

Present your bodies a living and holy sacrifice,
acceptable to God, which is your spiritual service of worship.
And do not be conformed to this world, but be
transformed by the renewing of your mind,
that you may prove what the will of God is,
that which is good and acceptable and perfect.
ROMANS 12:1–2

Mary had lived an exemplary life and was betrothed to Joseph. Then an angel came with an announcement that would cast a shadow of doubt on her impeccable character. God had asked Mary to bear His Son.

Leaving the results of this decision in the hands of her powerful God, Mary accepted her role as the mother of the Messiah. And during the difficult days that followed, she allowed the Word of God to renew her mind. But was that enough to give her sufficient power to obey the Lord?

The apostle Paul answers this question for us. "For though we walk in the flesh, we do not war according to the flesh, for the weapons of our warfare are not of the flesh, but divinely powerful for the destruction of fortresses. We are destroying speculations and every lofty thing raised up against the knowledge of God, and we are taking every thought captive to the obedience of Christ" (2 Corinthians 10:3–5).

The weapons God provides for us are spiritual. We must become proficient with such an arsenal before such can be effective. So, if the Lord says His Word is a weapon to be used against the enemy, we've got to read it, know it, and follow it.

Lord, I am grateful for Mary's example.

The Gathering at the Water Gate

And all the people gathered. . .at the square and
they asked Ezra the scribe to bring the book of the law
of Moses which the LORD had given to Israel.
Then Ezra the priest brought the law before the
assembly. . .on the first day of the seventh month.
And he read from it before the square. . . and all the
people were attentive to the book of the law.
NEHEMIAH 8:1–3

Through inspired teamwork, Nehemiah and the remnant of Israel finished rebuilding the wall in only fifty-two days (Nehemiah 6:15). Even their enemies lost the will to fight, recognizing this accomplishment as coming from the hand of Israel's God. Four times Sanballat and Geshem sent messages to Nehemiah, hoping to drag him away from finishing his task. And each time Nehemiah responded by saying, "'I am doing a great work and I cannot come down'" (Nehemiah 6:3). Sanballat accused Nehemiah of appointing prophets to proclaim that a king was in Judah.

Still, Nehemiah, refused to become agitated or frightened. Instead, he relied on God's strength. God put it in his heart "to assemble the nobles, the officials, and the people to be enrolled by genealogies. Then I found the book of the genealogy of those who came up first. . . from the captivity of the exiles whom Nebuchadnezzar the king of Babylon had carried away, and who returned to Jerusalem and Judah, each to his city" (Nehemiah 7:5–6). They searched for records prior to the captivity, to prove their lineage and family ties, but none could be found. In response, the people grieved.

Lord, let Nehemiah be an example of trust for me.

Amos the Prophet

Thus says the Lord, "For three transgressions of
Damascus and for four I will not revoke its punishment,
Because they threshed Gilead with implements of sharp
iron. . . I will also break the gate bar of Damascus,
and cut off the inhabitant from the valley of Aven,
and him who holds the scepter, from Betheden; So the
people of Syria will go exiled to Kir," Says the Lord.
Amos 1:3, 5

Throughout the Old Testament we've read accounts of God's wrath and fury directed toward those whom He loved who were flagrantly disobedient. But God also extended His loving hand of protection to those who walked in obedience.

Amos was a simple sheepherder from a small city about ten miles south of Jerusalem. He was called by God to deliver a warning to these stiff-necked, idol-worshiping people of the northern kingdom of Israel: "'I am not a prophet, nor am I the son of a prophet; for I am a herdsman and a grower of sycamore figs. But the Lord took me from following the flock and the Lord said to me, "Go prophesy to My people Israel"'" (Amos 7:14).

Contained within the nine chapters of this book is a list of the cities and peoples which God considers ripe for judgment, along with the specific warnings. As angry as God already was, He still gave these people two years to repent before the great earthquake came. Still, the people refused to listen.

Lord, thank You for Amos's prophecy : " 'Also I will
restore the captivity of My people Israel, And they
will rebuild the ruined cities and live in them' "
(Amos 9:14).

PHOEBE, SERVANT OF THE CHURCH

*I commend to you our sister Phoebe, who is a servant of
the church which is at Cenchrea; that you receive her in
the Lord in a manner worthy of the saints, and that you
help her in whatever matter she may have need of you;
for she herself has also been a helper of many,
and of myself as well.*

ROMANS 16:1–2

The apostle Paul singled Phoebe out as having been a great help both to the church at Cenchrea and to him personally. In bestowing this honor upon her, Paul showed to the ages the depth of Phoebe's Christian commitment.

Paul viewed dedicated people as living testimonies to all that God's Spirit could accomplish in one's character. Paul deeply appreciated those who walked in step with him to teach and nurture others in order to bring the Gospel message to many.

Paul also requested that other believers receive Phoebe "in a manner worthy of the saints." Obviously Christ within her shone out to others like a beacon of light to a needy world. And he asked that they assist her.

Some Bible translations also refer to her as a deaconess at the church in Cenchrea. At any rate, she was no ordinary woman.

Lord, as a woman, let my life, as Phoebe's, shine before others.

THE APPLE OF GOD'S EYE

*"For the day of the LORD draws near on all the nations.
As you have done, it will be done to you. Your dealings
will return on your own head. . . . Then the house of
Jacob will be a fire and the house of Joseph a flame; but
the house of Esau will be as stubble. And they will set
them on fire and consume them, so that there will be no
survivor of the house of Esau," for the LORD has spoken.*
OBADIAH 1:15, 18

Obadiah is such a tiny Old Testament book that
you've probably overlooked it. Yet there are prophecies and promises for Israel here that can't be missed.

Israel, the people God had chosen, began to feel
so overconfident that they considered themselves
invincible. But it wasn't this choosing which made
them special. Instead, it was the protection of God
that rendered them unique as a people. Now their
arrogance and lack of true worship rendered them
vulnerable to attack. Obadiah calls Israel back to worship their God, but also issues a warning to Edom,
the nation intent on wiping them out.

Scholars have divided opinions as to whether this
incident is referring to the time when the Philistines
and Arabs invaded Jerusalem in 853–841 BC, or
during the Babylonian sieges, between 605 and 586
BC. Closing the gap on this date is much less critical
than hearing the message.

*Lord, let me remember that it is Christ who is the head
of His Church and I am but a member of the Body.*

ESTHER IS CHOSEN

Then the king's attendants, who served him said,
"Let beautiful young virgins be sought for the king.
And let the king appoint overseers in all the provinces
of his kingdom that they may gather every beautiful
young virgin to Susa the capital, to the harem,
into the custody of Hegai, the king's eunuch,
who was in charge of the women; and let their cosmetics
be given them. Then let the young lady who pleases
the king be queen in place of Vashti."
ESTHER 2:2–4

The search was on for "the fairest maiden of them all."

The Book of Esther is a beautiful story of a woman's absolute faith and trust in her God. God placed Esther in a position of authority—in order to save the people of Israel.

Mordecai, a Jew in Susa, had returned from the Babylonian exile and was raising his orphaned niece, Esther. And she was "beautiful of form and face. . . Esther was taken to the king's palace" (Esther 2:5–8).

Wisely, "Esther did not make known her people or her kindred" (Esther 2:10). Esther lived in the ultimate spa resort where, for over twelve months, she received beauty treatments and perfume baths.

Finally, "Esther was taken to King Ahasuerus. . . And the king loved Esther more than all the women, and she found favor and kindness with him, so that he set the royal crown on her head and made her queen instead of Vashti" (Esther 2:16–17).

In the beginning, Esther was unaware of how God
would use her life. Lord, let me be as available and
obedient to You.

Jonah Flees God's Call

The word of the Lord came to Jonah the son of Amittai
saying, "Arise, go to Nineveh the great city, and cry against
it, for their wickedness has come up before Me." But Jonah
rose up to flee to Tarshish from the presence of the Lord.
So he went down to Joppa, found a ship which was going
to Tarshish, paid the fare, and went down into it to go
with them to Tarshish from the presence of the Lord.
Jonah 1:1–3

Jonah flat out didn't want this job, no way, no how! Therefore, he decided to "get out of Dodge." And the quickest route happened to be on the next boat sailing.

God had solicited Jonah's help in bringing a message to Nineveh. However, Jonah's fear of these Ninevites loomed far greater than his fear of the Lord.

But God always gives men and women a chance to change, and now He set about the task of getting Jonah's attention. First, "the Lord hurled a great wind on the sea and there was a great storm. . .so that the ship was about to break up" (Jonah 1:4). While the other passengers began frantically praying to their own gods as they threw the cargo overboard, Jonah went below and fell asleep.

"So the captain approached him and said, 'How is it that you are sleeping? Get up, call on your god. Perhaps your god will be concerned about us so that we will not perish'" (Jonah 1:6). What a joke! Jonah couldn't pray because he knew exactly who was causing this oceanic disturbance.

❧

Lord, I know that finally Jonah responded in faith.
Please help me take responsibility for the areas You're
ready to work on in my life.

Hearing God's Spirit Speak

For to us God revealed them through the Spirit; for the
Spirit searches all things, even the depths of God. . .
Now we have received, not the spirit of the world,
but the Spirit who is from God, that we might
know the things freely given to us by God.
1 Corinthians 2:10, 12

Have you ever tried to learn a foreign language? In high school I decided to take Spanish, and although I met the class requirements, I certainly didn't display unusual proficiency. Years later, God brought many Spanish-speaking people into my life. After taking a "Speed Spanish" course at the local junior college, my skills were rejuvenated enough so I could speak on a rudimentary level. Later I took a more in-depth class, and as long as I practiced, the ability to speak and understand Spanish came fairly easily.

This is exactly how to understand the things of God. You can't rely totally on what you received in your early education.

If you came to Christ as an adult then it's probably necessary to start from the beginning, using the Bible, not your memory. Find out what you believe and know why. If you never arrive at this understanding, how on earth can you share your faith with others?

Here's an excuse heard often: "We can't try to interpret the Bible ourselves because we'll get confused." But to refuse the Holy Spirit the opportunity to instruct you, as He promised He would, is to refuse true understanding.

Lord, fill my mind and heart with true understanding.

Esther Thwarts a Royal Plot

In those days, while Mordecai was sitting at the king's
gate, Bigthan and Teresh, two of the king's officials from
those who guarded the door, became angry and sought
to lay hands on King Ahasuerus. But the plot became
known to Mordecai, and he told Queen Esther,
and Esther informed the king in Mordecai's name.
ESTHER 2:21–22

Overhearing a private conversation in which a murder plot is discussed, Esther's uncle, Mordecai, a Jew, channeled this information back to his niece, whom the king trusted.

An official, Haman, had been promoted shortly after this incident had taken place. The king had commanded that all who were at the king's gate bow down and pay homage to Haman. However, Mordecai refused and "Haman was filled with rage" (Esther 3:5).

Therefore, Haman set an evil plan in motion. First came his accusation to the king: "'There is a certain people scattered and dispersed among the peoples in all the provinces of your kingdom; their laws are different from those of all other people, and they do not observe the king's laws, so it is not in the king's interest to let them remain'" (Esther 3:8).

Then Haman talked the king into issuing a decree that this people, the Jews, be destroyed. He even offered to pay 10,000 talents of silver to those who carried out what he termed as "'the king's business'" (Esther 3:9).

Lord, what a dark hour this was for Your people, but
You had already put a plan into action.

JONAH IS SWALLOWED BY A GREAT FISH

So they said to him, "What should we do to you that the
sea may become calm for us?"—for the sea was becoming
increasingly stormy. And he said to them, "Pick me up
and throw me into the sea. Then the sea will become
calm for you, for I know that on account of me this great
storm has come upon you." However, the men rowed
desperately to return to land but they could not, for the
sea was becoming even stormier against them.
JONAH 1:11–13

The storm-tossed sailors have two options, and neither one sounds like the right one.

Although these men were mad at Jonah for
involving them in his duel with God, they were also
aware that tossing him overboard like unwanted cargo
would almost certainly spell his death. It wasn't until
they had no other option that they finally complied
with his request.

All they could do now was hope that God
allowed him the time to live and speak. The sailors
even prayed to Jonah's God.

As soon as they threw Jonah into the water, the
sea stopped raging. "Then the men feared the Lord
greatly, and they offered a sacrifice to the Lord and
made vows. And the Lord appointed a great fish to
swallow Jonah, and Jonah was in the stomach of the
fish three days and three nights" (Jonah 1:16–17).

Lord, You alone have the ability to deliver a great fish to
swallow a man whole and not harm him. Help me trust
You for creative solutions to all my problems.

Our Bodies, God's Temple

Do you not know that you are a temple of God, and that the Spirit of God dwells in you? If any man destroys the temple of God, God will destroy him, for the temple of God is holy, and that is what you are.
1 CORINTHIANS 3:16–17

While people were living out the Old Testament times, God dwelt in His tabernacle. At first this was a traveling altar, known as the ark of the covenant, which the people carried with them from the time of Moses, through all the lands in which they wandered. When God's Son, Jesus Christ, came to earth He fulfilled God's requirements for sinful man through His death on the cross. Now God could cleanse man that He might indwell him, for God's temple is to be a holy place.

As we go about the business of life perhaps it's hard to remember that God indwells us. The apostle Paul constantly wrestled with desiring to do the right thing but having his flesh at war with his spirit. "For I know that nothing good dwells in me, that is, in my flesh; for the wishing is present in me, but the doing of the good is not. For the good that I wish, I do not do; but I practice the very evil that I do not wish" (Romans 7:18–19).

"However, you are not in the flesh but in the Spirit, if indeed the Spirit of God dwells in you. . . And if Christ is in you, though the body is dead because of sin, yet the spirit is alive because of righteousness" (Romans 8:9–10).

Lord, let me live as though I believe You are permeating my very being. Amen.

The Need for Godly Judges

Does any one of you, when he has a case against his neighbor, dare to go to law before the unrighteous, and not before the saints? Or do you not know that the saints will judge the world? If the world is judged by you, are you not competent to constitute the smallest law courts? Do you not know that we will judge angels? How much more matters of this life?

1 Corinthians 6:1–3

God meant for His Church to govern themselves so that true justice would be served. But He also intended that the believers work out their differences in love. Today men and women have quit counting on the power of God to rule in their lives and have turned instead to the "courts of the unbelievers," where they have not found justice.

Perhaps we should adjust the scales on the statue of the woman who has come to symbolize justice. Spend some time talking to people whose children have been victimized and you will find that their hearts were broken once by the initial crime and then all over again by the judicial system. Our laws must be rewritten with the victim in mind.

The verses above are meant to give you hope. For the saints of God will one day judge those who operate within this world system of injustice. As God brings down His own pair of legal scales to weigh and measure, they will be held accountable to Him.

Lord, help me remember the meaning of justice. May my court of law be governed by Your Holy Spirit in my heart.

QUEEN ESTHER'S SHINING MOMENT

"If I have found favor in the sight of the king, may the king and Haman come to the banquet which I shall prepare for them, and tomorrow I will do as the king says."
ESTHER 5:7–8

Haman dined with the king and queen. How prestigious! Then he went out of the gate and saw Mordecai, the Jew who refused to "tremble at his very presence."

"Haman controlled himself, however, went to his house, and sent for his friends and his wife Zeresh" (Esther 5:10). Then he recounted the glory of his riches, and every instance in which the king had magnified or promoted him. Last but not least, Haman bragged and gloated about having dined in the private audience of the king and queen (Esther 5:11–12). But it still bothered Haman that Mordecai wouldn't bow down to him. So Haman's wife suggested that he have a gallows prepared and hang Mordecai on it.

During the night the king couldn't sleep, so he grabbed the book of records and chronicles and had someone read them to him. And he found that Mordecai had never been properly honored for saving the king's life. The king called Haman and told him to make preparations for someone to receive a "royal honor." Haman was absolutely shocked when the king told him to bestow the gifts of a robe, crown, and horse on Mordecai.

At the second banquet she gave, Queen Esther finally related to the king the plot to kill all the Jews, reminding him of his promise to give her anything she desired.

Lord, thank You for giving Esther the wisdom and courage to save her people and Your people, the Jews.

ESTHER REQUESTS A NEW LAW

On that day King Ahasuerus gave the house of
Haman, the enemy of the Jews, to Queen Esther;
and Mordecai came before the king, for Esther had
disclosed what he was to her. . . And Esther set
Mordecai over the house of Haman. Then Esther spoke
again to the king, fell at his feet, wept, and implored
him to avert the evil scheme of Haman the Agagite
and his plot which he had devised against the Jews.
And the king extended the golden scepter to Esther.
So Esther arose and stood before the king.
ESTHER 8:1–4

When the king extended his scepter, it meant that
the person before him had permission to speak. And
Esther wasted no time in getting to the point. "If it
pleases the king. . .let it be written to revoke the letters devised by Haman, which he wrote to destroy the
Jews who are in all the king's provinces. For how can I
endure to see the calamity which shall befall my people, and how can I endure to see the destruction of my
kindred?'" (Esther 8:5–6)

Esther and Mordecai were among the few in
the king's palace who had acted in the king's behalf.
Everyone else desired personal gain. Esther had
risked her life not only for her people but also for the
king. Had it not been for God's intervention, Haman
undoubtedly would have hanged Esther on that gallows right along with Mordecai.

Lord, I thank You for this account of Esther's obedience,
loyalty, and trust.

MICAH KNEW HIS GOD

The word of the LORD which came to Micah... Hear,
O peoples, all of you; Listen, O earth and all it contains,
And let the LORD GOD be a witness against you,
the LORD from His holy temple. For behold, the LORD is
coming forth from His place. He will come down
and tread on the high places of the earth.
MICAH 1:1–3

Micah understood the Lord's awesome power. In fact, Micah's name means, "who is like Jehovah," forever reminding us that he understood the object of his faith. God used Micah to prophesy to the southern kingdom of Judah.

God's revelation to man was progressive. That's why it's so important to read the entire Bible, as each prophet unfolds another piece of God's end-time mystery. The events recorded in Micah would be fulfilled in the near and far-distant future.

"The mountains will melt under Him, And the valleys will be split, Like wax before the fire, Like water poured down a steep place. All this is for the rebellion of Jacob and for the sins of the house of Israel... For I will make Samaria a heap of ruins in the open country, Planting places for a vineyard. I will pour her stones down into the valley, And will lay bare her foundations" (Micah 1:4–6).

Why was God doing this to His people? Both Judah and Israel had forsaken their God, becoming steeped in idolatry.

Lord, keep me from following in the footsteps of the
rebellious that I might not require bitter lessons of truth.

The Preacher's Livelihood

*Who at any time serves as a soldier at his own
expense? Who plants a vineyard, and does not eat
the fruit of it? Or who tends a flock and does not
use the milk of the flock? I am not speaking these
things according to human judgment, am I?
Or does not the Law also say these things?*
1 Corinthians 9:7–8

Those who bring us the Word of God deserve a living wage. This is the point Paul is making. After all, the apostles had given up their homes and any semblance of normal family life in order to travel and present the Gospel. "Do we not have a right to eat and drink? Do we not have a right to take along a believing wife, even as the rest of the apostles, and the brothers of the Lord, and Cephas? Or do only Barnabas and I not have a right to refrain from working?" (1 Corinthians 9:4–6)

The word apostle means "one sent under commission." And if they had been called into service by God, weren't they entitled to the financial support from the body of believers? Paul chose to make tents for a living rather than have others support him.

So why did Paul choose to labor without receiving any wages? This way no one could accuse him of presenting the Gospel for personal gain. For Paul considered himself a servant for Jesus' sake (2 Corinthians 4:5).

Lord, let me remember in my prayers, tithes, and offerings all those who labor to bring the Word of God to me and others.

The Reason for Job's Suffering

Job. . .was blameless, upright, fearing God, and turning away from evil. Seven sons and three daughters were born to him. His possessions also were 7,000 sheep, 3,000 camels, 500 yoke of oxen, 500 female donkeys, and very many servants.
Job 1:1–3

This, of course, was life as Job used to know it, before his character was tested. "And the Lord said to Satan, 'Have you considered My servant Job? For there is no one like him on the earth, a blameless and upright man, fearing God and turning away from evil.' Then Satan answered the Lord, 'Does Job fear God for nothing? Hast Thou not made a hedge about him and his house. . .and all his possessions have increased in the land. But put forth Thy hand now and touch all that he has; he will surely curse Thee to Thy face'" (Job 1:8–11).

Satan intimated to God that Job only loved Him because of all the blessings Job had received. "Then the Lord said to Satan, 'Behold, all that he has is in your power, only do not put forth your hand on him'" (Job 1:12).

Job's life became an unwelcome ride on a trolley called tragedy. In one day he lost all his children and his house, servants, and livestock. And through all of this Job refused to blame God or sin.

Lord, as a Christian, lead me so that I do not expect You to be my "celestial Santa Claus." Lead me so I continue to follow, no matter the circumstances.

THE CONTENT OF OUR THOUGHTS

Woe to those who scheme iniquity, Who work out evil on their beds! When morning comes, they do it, For it is in the power of their hands. They covet fields and then seize them, And houses, and take them away. They rob a man and his house, A man and his inheritance.
MICAH 2:1–2

Micah acknowledges that the source of evil thoughts is the human mind. Other portions of Scripture also bear out this truth.

"Transgression speaks to the ungodly within his heart; There is no fear of God before his eyes. For it flatters him in his own eyes, Concerning the discovery of his iniquity and the hatred of it. The words of his mouth are wickedness and deceit; He has ceased to be wise and do good. He plans wickedness upon his bed; He sets himself on a path that is not good; He does not despise evil" (Psalm 36:1–4).

Therein lies the problem, that we at some point begin to accept wickedness as good. And the things we devise in our minds then become the vehicle for our actions.

Part and parcel of idolatrous worship, for which Israel as a nation assumed guilt before God, was that of human sacrifice to pagan gods. Can you understand why this sin was so detestable to the Lord?

Lord, guard my mind from evil that I might not ruminate on such things and be propelled into ungodly actions. Instead, let me turn to Your Word which acts as a cleansing agent.

GOD, JUDGE OF IMMORALITY PAST AND PRESENT

For I do not want you to be unaware, brethren, that our fathers were all under the cloud, and all passed through the sea; and all were baptized into Moses in the cloud and in the sea; and all ate the same spiritual food; and all drank the same spiritual drink, for they were drinking from a spiritual rock which followed them; and the rock was Christ. Nevertheless, with most of them God was not well-pleased; for they were laid low in the wilderness. Now these things happened as examples for us, that we should not crave evil things, as they also craved. . . Nor let us act immorally, as some of them did, and twenty-three thousand fell in one day.

1 CORINTHIANS 10:1–6, 8

By reading the entire Bible we have the privilege of learning from God's dealings with men and women throughout recorded history so we will not fall into the same traps. Twenty-three thousand people fell by the sword in one day because they joined themselves with pagan gods in sexual rituals, refusing to obey the true God.

How can we stop ourselves from falling into sin? By remembering: "No temptation has overtaken you but such as is common to man; and God is faithful, who will not allow you to be tempted beyond what you are able, but with the temptation will provide the way of escape also, that you may be able to endure it" (1 Corinthians 10:13).

Father, help me avoid temptation by taking one step closer to You.

183

The Holy Spirit, Our Great Gift

Therefore I make known to you that no one speaking by the Spirit of God says, "Jesus is accursed"; and no one can say, "Jesus is Lord," except by the Holy Spirit.

1 Corinthians 12:3

For twenty-nine years a desperate woman waded through the motions of life, wondering whether the Creator really cared for her at all. Her loneliness and despair seemed to confirm to her that He didn't. And then came the day when the Gospel message finally penetrated her soul with its extraordinary light and she began to call Him Lord.

I was that woman. When I heard today's Scripture the truth flew straight and sure as an arrow to the deepest part of my being.

It's no accident that despair caused me to succumb to messages of doubt concerning God's nature and character. The evil one is, after all, the author of confusion and lies. However, as I tested the spirits the truth became clear. "By this you know the Spirit of God: every spirit that confesses that Jesus Christ has come in the flesh is from God; and every spirit that does not confess Jesus is not from God; and this is the spirit of the antichrist, of which you have heard that it is coming, and now it is already in the world" (1 John 4:2–3).

Lord, I know if I'm listening to a message that makes me depressed and defeated, that's from Satan. I know the one that says I'm worth dying for is from Christ.

God Has Been There, Done That

*"It is God who removes the mountains. . .
Who alone stretches out the heavens, And tramples
down the waves of the sea; Who makes the Bear, Orion,
and the Pleiades, And the chambers of the south;
Who does great things, unfathomable,
And wondrous works without number."*
Job 9:5, 8–10

In one theology class I took, the teacher asked us to examine the ways in which we attempt to stuff God into a box. As A.W. Tozer said, "We tend to reduce God to manageable terms."

As our human nature cries out to control what we don't understand, this feat becomes impossible. For the God who has created all that we see, hear, touch, taste, and smell has been there and done that. When we accept this, our own importance seems diminished.

Even as Job screamed for relief from his pain, he recognized that both blessings and testing through trials flowed from the same loving hands. "'Your hands fashioned and made me altogether, And would You destroy me? Remember now, that You have has made me as clay; And would You turn me into dust again? You have granted me life and loving-kindness; And Your care has preserved my spirit'" (Job 10:8–9, 12).

I await the balm of good news from You, Lord. O may Your lovingkindness comfort me, "According to Your word to Your servant. May Your compassion come to me that I may live, For Your law is my delight" (Psalm 119:76–77).

What Response Does God Require?

With what shall I come to the LORD And bow myself before the God on high? . . . He has told you, O man, what is good; And what does the LORD require of you But to do justice, to love kindness, And to walk humbly with your God?
MICAH 6:6, 8

They drag themselves across the uneven pavement until their knees are bloodied and their exhausted bodies finally fall against the splintered wooden doors to the church. In this way, many in Mexico seek to do their yearly public penance for sin.

Christ has already paid the price that needed to be exacted for our sins. He took the whips, the lashes, the nailing to the cross, the verbal rebukes, and also the physical agony on our behalf. The God of this universe looked upon our futility and became a man, and then He sacrificed His life so that we who did not and could not ever deserve His mercy might obtain it. Jesus Christ did all this because He is both just and kind.

Isaiah prophesied the promise of Christ's cross. "Surely our griefs He Himself bore, And our sorrows He carried. . . But He was pierced through for our transgressions, He was crushed for our iniquities; The chastening for our well-being fell upon Him, And by His scourging we are healed" (Isaiah 53:4–5).

Though I expend every effort, I can never rid myself of sin. You've already provided the only way in which I can be cleansed.

His Fortunes Restored

The LORD restored the fortunes of Job when he prayed for his friends, and the LORD increased all that Job had twofold... The LORD blessed the latter days of Job more than his beginning, and he had 14,000 sheep, and 6,000 camels, and 1,000 yoke of oxen, and 1,000 female donkeys. And he had seven sons and three daughters.
Job 42:10, 12–13

Don't you just love stories with happy endings? Reading through the Book of Job makes anyone cry out for a great finish.

In today's Scripture, we join up again with Job's two friends. Well, the long arm of God's justice finally caught up with them and the Lord called them to accountability. "'Now therefore, take for yourselves seven bulls and seven rams, and go to My servant Job, and offer up a burnt offering for yourselves, and My servant Job will pray for you. For I will accept him so that I may not do with you according to your folly, because you have not spoken of Me what is right, as My servant Job has'" (Job 42:8).

Finally, Job received the Lord's public vindication. Revenge doesn't get any sweeter than that! And don't you know that Eliphaz and Temanite were "sweatin' it big time" as they awaited Job's eloquent prayer that would restrain God's hand of wrath!

Lord, through Job's pain, agony, and loss You placed "wisdom in his innermost being" concerning deep and marvelous truths about Your character. When I am afflicted, remind me to turn toward You.

Nahum Proclaims Israel's Restoration

Behold, on the mountains the feet of him who brings good news, Who announces peace! Celebrate your feasts, O Judah; Pay your vows. For never again will the wicked one pass through you; He is cut off completely.
Nahum 1:15

No news could be sweeter than the confirmation that a mighty enemy army was about to suffer a great demise. God gave Nahum, the prophet, just such a vision concerning the great Assyrian invaders who had devastated Judah. It had been such a long time that these pagans began boasting no god would be able to deliver the Israelites. However, the true God of power and might was now ready to act against them for enslaving His people. And they never saw it coming!

"The Lord takes vengeance on His adversaries, And He reserves wrath for His enemies. The Lord is slow to anger and great in power, And the Lord will by no means leave the guilty unpunished. . . Bashan and Carmel wither; The blossoms of Lebanon wither" (Nahum 1:2–4).

Nahum knows that if God is presenting a message then He's ready to take action. So Nahum, whose name means "comforter," is going to extol the virtues of His God to these pagans. That way, when God does begin His judgment, they'll know exactly whom they have encountered.

Lord, You are a mighty foe indeed! Why do people devise plots against You?

WHEN WILL OUR SUFFERING CEASE?

Blessed be the God and Father of our LORD Jesus Christ,
the Father of mercies and God of all comfort; who
comforts us in all our affliction so that we may be able to
comfort those who are in any affliction with the comfort
with which we ourselves are comforted by God. . . . But if
we are afflicted, it is for your comfort and salvation.
2 CORINTHIANS 1:3–4, 6

An experienced mountain biker and triathelete, my son hit some debris in the street when he was riding recently and, before he could dislodge his shoe clips, was thrown from his bike and onto a pile of bricks. His knee took the brunt of the fall, requiring surgery to repair the breaks.

Yet he seems to be taking this whole episode in stride, with a graciousness one wouldn't think possible. He and his fiancée have learned to depend upon each other in a new way: She is providing the medical expertise he desperately needs, while he has learned to allow her to intervene. And both of them depend entirely on the Lord's sufficiency.

This is the purpose of our trials, that we might comfort one another and lean on the Lord's strength. Paul's own burdens had been borne with a view of Christ that few of us will ever know.

Thank You, God, that in heaven all suffering will cease.

WHAT IS YOUR FOUNDATION?

"Woe to him who builds a city with bloodshed
And founds a town with violence!"
HABAKKUK 2:12

No matter how many westerns are made, we still flood into movie theaters to see them. We're fascinated that people survived for a time without food, water, and shelter to conquer the western frontier.

Yet the first western settlements were as much founded on religious beliefs as they were on bloodshed.

Blazing new territories isn't just about conquering the land. Martin Luther was pierced by a verse in Habakkuk and his reaction changed the course of church history. "'The righteous will live by his faith'" (Habakkuk 2:4). But in whom is this faith placed? If our faith is in Christ, we are established upon firm ground. But if it's in systems, programs, or even religion, it's doomed to fail.

The people of Judah were entering their darkest hour. The Babylonians had invaded this southern kingdom three times. During the final siege both Jerusalem and the temple were destroyed. Habakkuk is seeking assurance from the Lord that He will save them from extinction.

Thank You, God, for Your promise to Habakkuk:
" 'For the vision is yet for the appointed time; It hastens toward the goal, and it will not fail. Though it tarries, wait for it; For it will certainly come, it will not delay' "
(Habakkuk 2:3).

Paul's Trip to Paradise

*I know a man in Christ who fourteen years ago. . .was
caught up into Paradise, and heard inexpressible words,
which a man is not permitted to speak. On behalf of such
a man I will boast; but on my own behalf I will
not boast, except in regard to my weaknesses.*

2 Corinthians 12:2, 4–5

God propelled Paul up to heaven for a glimpse of
what was ahead for him and all believers.

But why does Paul present this vision as though
it happened to someone else? Remember that he had
been trained as a rabbi and had received a thorough
knowledge of the law. Rabbis often refer to themselves in the third person, to refrain from sounding
unduly prideful. Paul does clarify how he has handled
pride. "To keep me from exalting myself, there was
given me a thorn in the flesh, a messenger of Satan
to buffet me—to keep me from exalting myself!"
(2 Corinthians 12:7)

He never tells what that affliction was. But he did
understand it as coming from the Lord. Paul chose
not to dwell on his discomfort, clinging instead to the
incredible and unforgettable things he saw and heard
while in heaven.

*Lord, Your magnificent presence is all I need to provide
me with the momentum to continue spreading Your
Word.*

Whom Do You Follow, Moses or Christ?

Therefore, holy brethren, partakers of a heavenly calling, consider Jesus, the Apostle and High Priest of our confession. He was faithful to Him who appointed Him, as Moses also was in all His house. For He has been counted worthy of more glory than Moses, by just so much as the builder of the house has more honor than the house. For every house is built by someone, but the builder of all things is God.
HEBREWS 3:1–4

Do you ever wake up thinking about someone you may not have seen in years? Well, that's a "God call." God may be prompting your heart to respond to that person's need for encouragement.

One of Paul's great gifts was that of being an encourager. Yes, he spoke the truth unabashedly, yet he tempered it with praise and hope. "Therefore as you have received Christ Jesus the Lord, so walk in Him, having been firmly rooted and now being built up in Him and established in your faith, just as you were instructed, and overflowing with gratitude" (Colossians 2:6–7).

The writer of the Book of Hebrews spoke with the same conviction and understanding. "Encourage one another day after day, as long as it is still called 'Today,' lest any one of you be hardened by the deceitfulness of sin. For we have become partakers of Christ, if we hold fast the beginning of our assurance firm until the end" (Hebrews 3:13–14).

Man's memory of his own disobedience is so quickly forgotten, Lord. The opportunity to follow Christ lays before me. Lord, help me respond.

Who is the Rightful Heir?

Abraham had two sons, one by the bond woman and one by the free woman. The son by the bondwoman was born according to the flesh, and the son by the free woman through the promise.

GALATIANS 4:22–23

Sibling rivalry is at the crux of the quarrel between the Arabs and Israelis. Both peoples claim Abraham as their father and therefore feel entitled to his inheritance. However, God Himself made a great distinction between the two, calling Isaac the "son of promise" and Ishmael "the son of the slave woman."

God had promised Abraham a son but at eighty-six years old, Abraham had become weary of waiting (Genesis 16:16). To him, it was apparent that Sarah, his wife, was barren. So, at Sarah's urging, Abraham sought out the slave girl Hagar, and she conceived. Abraham's action led to much dissension within his home. And by the time Sarah conceived the son of promise, the household was in a complete upheaval. God promised to make both sides great nations (Genesis 21:9–13).

Paul now uses these two sons to illustrate the status of the unbeliever versus her changed relationship once she commits her life to Christ. Once we were slaves to sin. But with our redemption in Christ we become free.

Lord, through the line of Isaac men and women are truly blessed. For Christ Himself would be that seed from whom Redemption would come (Galatians 3:13–18).

The Fruit of the Spirit

But the fruit of the Spirit is love, joy, peace, patience,
kindness, goodness, faithfulness, gentleness, self-control;
against such things there is no law. Now those who
belong to Christ Jesus have crucified the flesh with
its passions and desires. If we live by the Spirit,
let us also walk by the Spirit.
Galatians 5:22–25

When we become Christians we receive spiritual gifts as a result of our inward relationship with Jesus Christ. These gifts are known in the Bible as the fruit of the Spirit, but what does that really mean?

Inventoried in today's Scripture are qualities that, apart from God's power, would likely not be displayed in our character.

Take, for instance, joy. How many truly joyful people do you know? Most of us could probably count them on one hand. Joy is the inward peace and sufficiency that transcends life's circumstances.

So, what's the catch? Why is God showering us with these gifts? Because they prove that He can enter a human life and affect her or him with change, that others might also be won to Christ as they observe this miracle.

Lord, my greatest gift from You is salvation, Your grace
enables me to begin life with a fresh start. And with
this transformation of character, fruit becomes the yield,
shared as I serve the body of believers with my unique
spiritual gifts.

JAMES, BOND-SERVANT OF GOD

James, a bond-servant of God and of the Lord Jesus Christ, to the twelve tribes who are dispersed abroad: Greetings. Consider it all joy, my brethren, when you encounter various trials, knowing that the testing of your faith produces endurance.
JAMES 1:1–3

As the Lord's half-brother, James had observed the life of Christ from a close vantage point, yet missed entirely the fact that someone within his own family was the Messiah.

Like so many others, James had taken Christ for granted. Jesus' sinless life had been lived out before him and yet James had not responded to the invitation for salvation.

James finally understood his position in Christ, that of a servant. He had successfully journeyed from a place of hindering the Gospel, unaware of the time constraints Christ had with the Father, to a place of understanding the true source of wisdom (John 7:1–5). The apostle Paul relates that James, along with Peter and John, became one of the chief leaders of the church in Jerusalem (Galatians 2:9).

How grateful I am, Lord, that You're not willing that any should perish, especially those of Your own family.

WHAT CONSTITUTES DYNAMIC FAITH?

You believe that God is one. You do well; the demons
also believe, and shudder. But are you willing to
recognize, you foolish fellow, that faith without works is
useless? Was not Abraham our father justified by works,
when he offered up Isaac his son on the altar?
You see that faith was working with his works,
and as a result of the works, faith was perfected; and
the Scripture was fulfilled which says, "And Abraham
believed God, and it was reckoned to him as righteous-
ness," and he was called the friend of God.
JAMES 2:19–23

Abraham's faith was evident by his actions. The very foundation of Abraham's faith was the Word of God. And no matter what God required of him, Abraham obeyed God. Therefore, all of his actions were born out of the call God had on his life.

"Faith comes from hearing, and hearing by the word of Christ" (Romans 10:17). This kind of dynamic faith involves the whole person. If someone professes their belief in God and yet does not take the Word to others, and does not attend a weekly Bible study, and can't be bothered to help those in obvious need, it makes me wonder whether that faith is real. For there has to be some outward manifestation of the change that takes place inwardly.

Lord, show me by Your Word how to reflect dynamic faith.

Sealed by the Holy Spirit

In Him, you also, after listening to the message of truth,
the gospel of your salvation—having also believed,
you were sealed in Him with the Holy Spirit of promise,
who is given as a pledge of our inheritance,
with a view to the redemption of God's own
possession, to the praise of His glory.
Ephesians 1:13–14

Ornamental sealing waxes and metal impressions were used in the past as both a security measure and a statement of authenticity, especially by royalty. The king's signet ring was pressed into the hot melted wax, leaving an indelible and unique impression. Paul was inspired to use this image to describe how we, as believers, are sealed by God's Holy Spirit.

The apostle Paul penned the Book of Ephesians between AD 60 to 62 while he was a prisoner in Rome. Ephesus, the fourth largest city in the Roman Empire, was steeped in idolatrous worship.

Into this spiritual darkness God sent Paul. The Lord desired to use this cultural setting to call out for Himself a church so that He could shine the light of truth upon this evil place.

Lord, there are dark places today that cry out for Your redeeming light. Lead me to share Your Word where it is needed desperately.

A Husband's Love

Wives, be subject to your own husbands, as to the Lord.
For the husband is the head of the wife, as Christ also is
the head of the church, He Himself being the Savior of
the body. But as the church is subject to Christ, so also
the wives ought to be to their husbands in everything.
EPHESIANS 5:22–24

Wives, our role is that of a helpmate, not doormat. It's critical to remember that God intended marriage to be a partnership. Thus, if each person vies for control, the union begins eroding until it simply dissolves. Instead, we need to build one another up.

"So husbands ought also to love their own wives as their own bodies. He who loves his own wife loves himself; for no one ever hated his own flesh, but nourishes and cherishes it, just as Christ also does the church, because we are members of His body" (Ephesians 5:28–29). If men truly loved their wives to this degree, there probably isn't a woman alive who'd run from it.

So what can we do to make things better? Pray. . . every single day. But especially when things are out of kilter. Know that God is vitally interested in the success of your marriage and act accordingly.

Lord, I know that only You are capable of loving per-
fectly. So the next time my marriage feels like a 90/10
proposition, please remind me that You're giving 100
percent.

Peter, an Apostle of Jesus Christ

*Peter, an apostle of Jesus Christ, to those who reside as
aliens. . .who are chosen according to the foreknowledge
of God the Father, by the sanctifying work of the Spirit,
that you may obey Jesus Christ and be sprinkled with His
blood: May grace and peace be yours in fullest measure.*
1 Peter 1:1–2

The only true "superhero" is Jesus Christ, who will
never fail us. He alone was fully God and fully man.
Therefore, He alone possesses perfectly all the char-
acteristics we most admire. For He remains faithful,
just, loving, omnipotent, and eternal.

To credit Peter with a more elevated status
than the one given to him by Christ is to add to the
Scriptures. By his own admission Peter was the apostle to the Jews, just as Paul was the apostle to the
Gentiles, and upon neither was the title "head of the
church" conferred. Christ alone holds that title. "For
the husband is the head of the wife, as Christ also is
the head of the church, He Himself being the Savior
of the body" (Ephesians 5:23).

Peter never seeks position or power. Instead, he
humbly admonishes his hearers to "obey Christ," on
whom Peter also depends.

*The name Peter, or petra, means "rock." Help my faith,
Lord, to be rock solid and unwavering.*

The Meaning of True Christian Fellowship

I thank my God in all my remembrance of you, always offering prayer with joy in my every prayer for you all, in view of your participation in the gospel from the first day until now. . . For it is only right for me to feel this way about you all, because I have you in my heart, since both in my imprisonment and in the defense and confirmation of the gospel, you all are partakers of grace with me.

PHILIPPIANS 1:3–5, 7

Paul was confined to prison when he wrote his letter to the Philippians. Yet rather than wallowing in self-pity, we see him reaching out to those he loves and reminiscing about their joyful times of fellowship together. The sheer memory of them causes warmth to invade his lonely prison. And though he longs to be with them, he is content in the place Christ has called him.

Paul's joy is not dependent upon circumstances. Rather, it overflows from the content of his heart, where the true source of joy resides, Jesus Christ. And because of this indwelling, Paul senses a oneness with other believers, despite the fact that they are far from him. It is the love of Christ that binds them together.

Paul's only aim in life was to be where God wanted him—so that he might spread the Gospel to all who would listen. And if this aspiration required suffering and isolation on his part, then Paul gladly paid the price.

Lord, might I pray as Paul, "I press on toward the goal for the prize of the upward call of God in Christ Jesus" (Philippians 3:14).

$\mathcal{B}$EING OF $\mathcal{O}$NE $\mathcal{M}$IND

*Do nothing from selfishness or empty conceit, but
with humility of mind let each of you regard one
another as more important than yourselves; do not
merely look out for your own personal interests,
but also for the interests of others.*

PHILIPPIANS 2:3–4

While vacationing in the Midwest this past fall, my husband and I toured several Amish communities. How well these people live out the teaching of today's Scripture on unity. Forsaking the modern world that surrounds them, with a deep sense of community, the Amish labor together for the good of all.

As Christians we are called to encourage one another in the faith. Paul, who spent so much of his own life in prison, had a deep understanding of the need for the reassurance and hope, which the Lord richly supplied. This reliance on God's abundant source of blessings overflowed from his heart, spilling out to his fellow Christians.

What if we used the greeting time in church, during the worship service, to find out the specific needs within the Body of Christ? Many of our brothers and sisters are wounded, both physically and spiritually. Yet they come to Sunday services with a deceptive smile on their faces, their return trip home as lonely as the rest of their week will probably be. Do you care?

Who is my source of strength? Lord, help me encourage others.

STAND FIRM AND RECEIVE THE CROWN

Therefore, my beloved brethren whom I long to see,
my joy and crown, so stand firm in the Lord, my
beloved. I urge Euodia and I urge Syntyche
to live in harmony in the Lord.
PHILIPPIANS 4:1–2

Church committee meetings can either be a blessing or a bear, depending, of course, upon whether the members are working together for a common goal. Evidently, two of the church women at Philippi, Euodia and Syntyche, were less than harmonious. Therefore, Paul admonished them.

It is significant that Paul took the time to address this issue. Left unchecked, such arguing would wreak havoc in the church. Perhaps you have encountered someone who, although she professes belief in Christ, has treated you without charity or love. Fast, pray for guidance, and then go to her and pray again. Failure to do so gives Satan an opportunity to get a foothold within the church, as the argument escalates and people choose sides.

Speaking like a proud father, Paul refers to these believers at Philippi as his "joy and crown." He brought the Gospel message to them. And then he stood back to watch them grow in their faith. He doesn't want it all to turn to ashes.

Lord, help me to remember that You surrendered all Your rights that I might know true freedom. Please show me how to persevere, make amends, and live in harmony.

WHERE IS THE PROMISE OF HIS COMING?

Know this first of all, that in the last days mockers will
come with their mocking, following after their own lusts,
and saying "Where is the promise of his coming? For
ever since the fathers fell asleep, all continues just as
it was from the beginning of creation." For when they
maintain this, it escapes their notice that by the word
of God the heavens existed long ago and the earth was
formed out of water by water; through which the world
at that time was destroyed, being flooded with water.

2 PETER 3:3–6

If you aren't into eschatology, or the study of events
to come at the end of time, perhaps you won't share
my appreciation of this verse. However, here's Peter,
over 2,000 years ago, letting us know that the earth
we know will someday be destroyed. How will this
happen?

"But by His word the present heavens and earth
by His word are being reserved for fire, kept for the
day of judgment and destruction of ungodly men"
(2 Peter 3:7).

How can a loving God destroy the very men and
women and their world He created? Look at how
much time He provided for them to repent. From
the time Noah received the order from God to build
the ark until the rain began, a span of 120 years had
elapsed. Certainly this was time enough for everyone
to hear the prediction and take appropriate action.

Today I will repent of my sins. And, if I'm not entirely
sure I've done so, today I will claim Jesus to be my Savior
and Lord.

God Stands by His Word

God always keeps His promises. Through Moses, God had warned the nation of Israel that if they refused to obey, they would be taken into captivity. In 586 BC this prophecy was fulfilled.

God spoke through the prophet Jeremiah, giving the exact duration of this captivity as seventy years. This is the number of years Israel remained in Babylon.

Today's Scripture reveals two specific messages. First, a messenger will precede Messiah, announcing Him to Israel. This would be John the Baptist (Luke 1:76).

Next, the Messiah will "come to His temple." Three specific times stand out from the rest. At the time of His circumcision a prophecy was given about Christ being the appointed child by Simeon (Luke 2:34). When He was twelve years old he became separated from Mary and Joseph when they were preparing to leave Jerusalem. They found Him in the temple, astounding the learned scholars about His knowledge of Scripture (Luke 2:42–51). The third time Christ stood in the temple and read from the Book of Isaiah the very prophecy concerning His coming. Then He said, "Today this Scripture has been fulfilled in your hearing" (Luke 4:21).

*Jesus Christ, God's promise to the world, has come!
Thank You for Your Word of Truth.*

Hold to God's Truth, Not to Visions

You have died and your life is hidden with Christ in God. When Christ, who is our life, is revealed, then you also will be revealed with Him in glory. Therefore consider the members of your earthly body as dead to immorality, impurity, passion, evil desire, and greed, which amounts to idolatry. For it is on account of these things that the wrath of God will come upon the sons of disobedience, and in them you also once walked, when you were living in them.
Colossians 3:3–7

Some Christian testimonies really stir your heart. Some are from individuals who have turned from lives of debauchery and waste to become true seekers of God.

Our churches are comprised of redeemed sinners. "For all have sinned and fall short of the glory of God, being justified as a gift by His grace through the redemption which is in Christ Jesus; whom God displayed publicly as a propitiation in His blood through faith" (Romans 3:23–25).

Paul's message is that Christ in us should cause a change in our lives. For we have been delivered from the "wrath of God." This metamorphosis should make a visible difference in how we are living our lives. For Christ has set up residence within us.

There cannot be any detours or distractions from the truth. "Let no one keep defrauding you of your prize by delighting in self-abasement and the worship of the angels" (Colossians 2:18).

Let me be cautious of bypassing the Word of God and the Spirit of God to substitute visions of angels for the Gospel.

CHRIST ELIMINATED ALL ETHNIC BARRIERS

*There is no distinction between Greek and Jew,
circumcised and uncircumcised, barbarian, Scythian,
slave and freeman, but Christ is all, and in all. So, as
those who have been chosen of God, holy and beloved,
put on a heart of compassion, kindness, humility,
gentleness and patience; bearing with one another and
forgiving each other, whoever has a complaint against
anyone; just as the Lord forgave you, so also should you.*
COLOSSIANS 3:11–13

To say we love Christ and yet maintain deeply rooted prejudices against others is inconsistent with everything He taught. For Christ came to reconcile all peoples to Himself, not separate us into factions.

Above all, God wants us to be harmonious in worship of Him and also in working with Him. "Now may the God who gives perseverance and encouragement grant you to be of the same mind with one another according to Christ Jesus; that with one accord you may with one voice glorify the God and Father of our Lord Jesus Christ. Wherefore, accept one another, just as Christ also accepted us to the glory of God" (Romans 15:5–7).

Lord, let the true peace of Christmas, which is Christ, be found in my heart as I am obedient to Your command to love one another, just as You have loved me (John 13:34).

The Father has Bestowed a Great Love

See how great a love the Father has bestowed upon
us, that we should be called children of God; and such
we are. For this reason the world does not know us,
because it did not know Him. Beloved, now we are
children of God, and it has not appeared as yet what
we will be. We know that when He appears, we will
be like Him, because we will see Him just as He is.
And everyone who has this hope fixed on Him
purifies himself, just as He is pure.
1 John 3:1–3

Have you ever looked into the mirror and thought, *I wish I had a new body?* Well, Christ has one reserved for you in heaven. This body is imperishable, undefiled, and will not fade away (1 Peter 1:3–4).

While we don't know when Jesus is coming again, we do know that our new bodies will coincide with this event. "When Christ, who is our life, is revealed, then you also will be revealed with Him in glory" (Colossians 3:4).

Yet the gift of our new bodies is only one aspect of the Father's incredible love for His children. His love prompts His children to purify themselves just as He is pure (1 John 3:3). They also abide in Him and practice righteousness (1 John 3:6–7), for they have been born of God (1 John 3:9; John 3:7).

Lord, as I prepare to celebrate Your birth, the greatest gift I can lay beside the manger is an act of my will that makes me Your child. Yes, I have been born again.

HE IS COMING WITH THE CLOUDS

Behold, He is coming with the clouds, and every eye will see Him, even those who pierced Him; and all the tribes of the earth will mourn over Him. So it is to be. Amen.
REVELATION 1:7

Cecil B. DeMille was known for his extravagant movie productions. Who can forget his version of Moses parting the Red Sea? However, the appearance of Christ in the clouds will surpass every event that has ever taken place on earth. This future event will be a worldwide phenomenon in which every eye will see Him. And the hearts of those who refused to examine the evidence and refused to know Him will ache with the agonizing pain of conviction that it's simply too late. The purpose for His appearance this time will be to judge the world of its greatest sin, the rejection of His great gift of salvation.

Those who are "unprepared" for this global happening will be in shock! "For the Lord Himself will descend from heaven with a shout, with the voice of the archangel, and with the trumpet of God, and the dead in Christ will rise first. Then we who are alive and remain shall be caught up together with them in the clouds to meet the Lord in the air, and so we shall always be with the Lord" (1 Thessalonians 4:16–17). It doesn't get any better than this!

Father, when humans have failed me, I tend to blame You for their choices. Please break down the barriers in my heart that I might worship Your Son this Christmas.

SPIRIT OF GOD OR SPIRIT OF ANTICHRIST?

The eyes of the Lord are toward the righteous,
And His ears are open to their cry.
PSALM 34:15

When those inevitable disagreements occur between husband and wife, they are often accompanied by a time of lost fellowship and an intense sense of isolation. Yesterday found me sitting alone on a huge boulder in the mountain retreat where we were camped. I cried out to God for intervention, that He might "fix this man," but God seemed absolutely silent. After forty minutes or so I got up and returned to our campsite, knowing that God would somehow work out this rift.

This morning I read the following Scripture: "For the eyes of the Lord are upon the righteous, and His ears attend to their prayer, But the face of the Lord is against those who do evil" (1 Peter 3:12). The Spirit of God heard my cry and took my petition before the Father who answered my prayer, for I have confessed belief in Him.

If you have discarded the commands of God, then you are not God's child. "You are from God, little children, and have overcome them; because greater is He who is in you than he who is in the world. They are from the world; therefore they speak as the world, and the world listens to them" (1 John 4:4–5).

Lord, guide me in this last hour, that I continue to spread the Gospel and not walk away.

GOD'S MESSAGE TO THE CHURCHES

> " 'But I have this against you, that you
> have left your first love.' "
> REVELATION 2:4

One of my favorite questions to ask couples over dinner is "How did you meet?" Each story invariably presents a set of impossible circumstances that had to be orchestrated in order to bring this man and woman together. As these details are relayed, a glow begins to come back into the eyes of those remembering. There is nothing to compare with that "first bloom of love."

This is the kind of love God desires from us. That on-fire, totally consuming, single focus of our attention. His call to the church at Ephesus then was that they remember their first love—and rekindle their purpose to seek Him first.

His message, however, to the church at Smyrna was very different. "'I know your tribulation and your poverty (but you are rich). Do not fear what you are about to suffer. . . Be faithful until death, and I will give you the crown of life'" (Revelation 2:9–10).

Throughout history, God's church has suffered persecution. But here is a message of hope to all for whom cruelty is a constant companion: "Remain faithful, God's reward is at hand."

O Lord, may Your Light be the fire in my soul!

Those Born of God Obey Him

*Whoever believes that Jesus is the Christ is born of God;
and whoever loves the Father loves the child born of
Him. By this we know that we love the children of God,
when we love God and observe His commandments.*

1 John 5:1–2

When our children disobey, we feel not only extreme disappointment but also a sense that they don't love us. For if they did, they would understand that our instructions are meant to guide them over the rough terrain of life. This is exactly how God feels when we fail to follow Him. For He equates love with obedience.

"'If you love Me, you will keep My commandments'" (John 14:15). How on earth can we accomplish this task? By the power of God's Spirit within us! "'And I will ask the Father, and He will give you another Helper, that He may be with you forever; that is the Spirit of truth'" (John 14:16–17).

How can we know for sure that the Spirit of God indwells us? "And the witness is this, that God has given us eternal life, and this life is in His Son. He who has the Son has the life; he who does not have the Son of God does not have the life" (1 John 5:11–12).

Lord, if I'm wandering without purpose, please bring me close to You. Help me make room in my heart for the Babe of Christmas!

WHEN WILL CHRIST RAPTURE THE FAITHFUL?

*Now we request you, brethren, with regard to the coming
of our Lord Jesus Christ and our gathering together to
Him, that you may not be quickly shaken from your
composure or be disturbed either by a spirit or a message
or a letter as if from us, to the effect that the day of the
Lord has come. Let no one in any way deceive you, for
it will not come unless the apostasy comes first, and the
man of lawlessness is revealed, the son of destruction,
who opposes and exalts himself above every so-called god
or object of worship, so that he takes his seat in the temple of God, displaying himself as being God.*
2 THESSALONIANS 2:1–4

Paul and Timothy had founded the church at
Thessalonica. For a time these Thessalonians
remained strong. But then came persecution so severe
that they were shaken to their roots. If these tri-
al-filled days comprised their last moments on earth,
where was the hope of being "caught up in Christ"?
Had they somehow missed it all?

Paul wanted to dispel their misconceptions and
correct several weaknesses in this church.

Before the antichrist bursts onto the world scene,
there will be a great falling away from the truth:
"Some will fall away from the faith, paying attention to deceitful spirits and doctrines of demons, by
means of the hypocrisy of liars seared in their own
conscience as with a branding iron, men who forbid
marriage and advocate abstaining from foods, which
God has created to be gratefully shared in by those
who believe and know the truth" (1 Timothy 4:1–3).

Even so, come Lord Jesus!

The Father Has Commanded Us to Love

The elder to the chosen lady and her children, whom I love in truth; and not only I, but also all who know the truth, for the sake of the truth which abides in us and will be with us forever: Grace, mercy and peace will be with us, from God the Father and from Jesus Christ, the Son of the Father, in truth and love.

2 John 1:1–3

A foundation of any small-group home Bible study should be the love members display toward one another. It was just such a group that John addressed in this letter.

As a church elder, John reminded these believers that God didn't consider loving one another an option. John further expounded on this concept, viewing it from God's perspective. "And this is love, that we walk according to his commandments" (2 John 1:6).

John shows us the process by which the Word of the Lord can penetrate our hearts. First, we are to know the truth, (2 John 1:1–3), for it is by God's grace that we can love others.

Next, John admonishes us to walk according to His commandments (John 1:4–6).

Last, we must abide in the truth, who is Christ (2 John 1:7–11). Jesus said, "'I am the way, and the truth, and the life; no one comes to the Father, but through Me'" (John 14:6).

Jesus Christ. . .heralded by a star, proclaimed by angels, announced by the shepherds, and given by the Father to a world in need of a Savior. O, come let me adore Him!

Jesus Alone is Worthy

I saw in the right hand of Him who sat on the throne
a book written inside and on the back, sealed up with
seven seals. And I saw a strong angel proclaiming with
a loud voice, "Who is worthy to open the book and
to break its seals? . . ." Then I began to weep greatly,
because no one was found worthy to open the book,
or to look into it; and one of the elders said to me,
"Stop weeping; behold, the Lion that is from the tribe
of Judah, the Root of David, has overcome so as
to open the book and its seven seals."
REVELATION 5:1–2, 4–5

As the Lamb stood to receive "the book," an awed hush fell over His celestial audience. For He alone was worthy, because He had met God's requirements to redeem the earth. The prize was His. "While He had taken the book, the four living creatures and the twenty-four elders fell down before the Lamb, holding each one a harp and golden bowls full of incense, which are the prayers of the saints. And they sang a new song, saying, 'Worthy are You to take the book, and to break its seals; for You were slain, and purchased for God with Your blood men from every tribe and tongue and people and nation'" (Revelation 5:8–9).

The judgments of God comprise the book. These are a series of progressively worsening catastrophes, deserved by those who have consistently rejected God, salvation in Christ, and His Word.

Lord, I know I can't truly celebrate Christmas unless I know that Jesus Christ is God in the flesh, born to die on the cross for my sins. Because of His sacrifice I will be able to celebrate forever with Him in heaven.

Jesus Christ, Our Hope

To Timothy, my true child in the faith: Grace,
mercy and peace from God the Father and Christ
Jesus our Lord. As I urged you upon my departure for
Macedonia, remain on at Ephesus, in order that you
may instruct certain men not to teach strange doctrines,
nor to pay attention to myths and endless genealogies,
which give rise to mere speculation rather than furthering
the administration of God which is by faith. But the goal
of our instruction is love from a pure heart and a good
conscience and a sincere faith.

1 Timothy 1:2–5

Paul wrote this letter to encourage Timothy in his own leadership role, knowing that the worst thing this young believer could do was to try and emulate Paul instead of Christ. For Paul held no doubt in his mind concerning Timothy's call from God. "This command I entrust to you, Timothy, my son, in accordance with the prophecies previously made concerning you, that by them you may fight the good fight, keeping faith and a good conscience, which some have rejected and suffered shipwreck in regard to their faith" (1 Timothy 1:18–19). Paul continues with this powerful admonition: "Do not neglect the spiritual gift within you, which was bestowed upon you through prophetic utterance with the laying on of hands by the presbytery" (1 Timothy 4:14).

Timothy is his "true child in the faith," for Paul had led him to Christ and never ceased to pray for his spiritual growth.

◈

Lord, show me how to use my special gifts.

JESUS CHRIST CAME IN THE FLESH

Anyone who goes too far and does not abide in the teaching of Christ, does not have God; the one who abides in the teaching, he has both the Father and the Son. If anyone comes to you and does not bring this teaching, do not receive him into your house, and do not give him a greeting; for the one who gives him a greeting participates in his evil deeds.

2 JOHN 1:9–11

There is no greater evil than to fail to recognize who Jesus Christ is, God in the flesh. God has tried from the beginning of time to build a bridge to humankind. He gave men and women His laws and yet they failed to obey. Then the Lord sent His prophets. But the people refused to listen. And finally, He sent Jesus, to show us how to live upon the earth. And instead of responding to His offer of salvation, men nailed Him to a cross.

Today's Scripture warns against false teachings. The apostle Paul also issued an urgent caution: "Now I urge you, brethren, keep your eye on those who cause dissensions and hindrances contrary to the teaching which you learned, and turn away from them. For such men are slaves, not of our Lord Christ but of their own appetites; and by their smooth and flattering speech they deceive the hearts of the unsuspecting" (Romans 16:17–18).

Lord, strengthen my faith so that I can love those who don't know You, so that I can reveal the true identity of Your Son.

ORDER IN OUR PRAYERS

First of all, then, I urge that entreaties and prayers,
petitions and thanksgivings, be made on behalf of all
men, for kings and all who are in authority, so that
we may lead a tranquil and quiet life in all godliness
and dignity. This is good and acceptable in the sight of
God our Savior, who desires all men to be saved
and to come to the knowledge of the truth.
1 TIMOTHY 2:1–4

The demands of this world, and the pace at which our technology is racing, can sometimes overwhelm us, causing feelings of panic, powerlessness, and even paranoia. Is there a solution that brings life back into perspective? Yes. And God calls it prayer.

Our human sense of ineptness—we simply aren't equal to the task of being in charge of the universe—causes us to react to pressure. So, we've got to release the hand controls back to God. And when we practice this on an individual level, the prayers we offer within our congregations become more effective.

Prayer isn't some mystical entity to be attained by a few saintly little ladies in the church. Instead, it is an act of worship on the part of the created toward the Creator. Prayer is simply "talking to God" about everything that affects our lives.

Spirit of God, fall afresh on me that I might lift my voice
in petition to You.

Welcoming Other Believers

The elder to the beloved Gaius, whom I love in truth. . .
Beloved, you are acting faithfully in whatever you accom-
plish for the brethren, and especially when they
are strangers; and they have testified to your love
before the church. You will do well to send
them on their way in a manner worthy of God.
3 JOHN 1:1, 5–6

Gaius, a strong and cordial believer, was dearly loved by the apostle John. We see in today's Scripture that John refers to him as "beloved." Gaius extended a hand of loving fellowship to all who came to worship. But it was the truth to which Gaius was a witness that had molded this extraordinary life, one centered on obedience to God. Gaius provided genuine hospitality. And evidently this included opening his own home, heart, and pocketbook to others, that the Word of God might go forth.

If only we all might have such pure motives for assisting others, that they might receive God's Word and see His love flowing all around them. Such a practical ministry of serving God gives honor to God, is a penetrating witness to the lost, and is a way of demonstrating obedience to God.

Father, my church will likely be filled this Christmas with people who may only "press the flesh with the faithful" once or twice a year. May I give these inquiring minds a warm reception.

Paul's Ministry Comes to a Close

*Paul, an apostle of Christ Jesus by the will of God,
according to the promise of life in Christ Jesus, to
Timothy, my beloved son. . . I constantly remember you
in my prayers night and day, longing to see you, even
as I recall your tears, so that I may be filled with joy.
For I am mindful of the sincere faith within you, which
first dwelt in your grandmother Lois, and your mother
Eunice, and I am sure that it is in you as well.*

2 TIMOTHY 1:1, 3–5

One of my favorite full-time jobs was keeping a database for a large magazine publisher. However, as time went on I became more convinced that the Lord was calling me away to begin my own ministry of writing. Training my replacement hurt my soul to the core.

As I read Paul's second letter to Timothy, I can identify with his anguish at letting go. Paul had to make sure that Timothy, who suffered from bouts of insecurity, remained strong in the faith. For Timothy would now "carry the torch of faith" and continue bringing the Gospel to all who would listen.

Paul praises Timothy, reminding him of the heritage of belief passed down to him from his mother, Eunice, and grandmother, Lois. And Paul, the ever-present spiritual mentor, expresses his love by referring to Timothy as "my beloved son."

Use me, Lord, to do Your will.

THE ETERNAL GOSPEL

*"And I saw another angel flying in midheaven,
having an eternal gospel to preach to those who live on
the earth, and to every nation and tribe and tongue and
people; and he said with a loud voice, 'Fear God, and
give Him glory, because the hour of His judgment has
come; and worship Him who made the heaven and
the earth and the sea and springs of waters.' "*

REVELATION 14:6–7

Following the Resurrection, Jesus prepared to leave
this earth and return to heaven. Before going, He
delivered a message to His disciples and charged
them with a mission: "Go therefore and make disciples of all the nations, baptizing them in the name of
the Father and the Son and the Holy Spirit, teaching
them to observe all that I commanded you; and lo,
I am with you always, even to the end of the age"
(Matthew 28:19–20).

This great commission is extended to all who
choose to believe in Christ. In looking for creative
ways to present the Good News to the children who
visit my home, I filled a large, handmade bag with
age-appropriate books and videos. How eagerly the
kids seek out this "grandma bag," ready to discover
more about the Lord.

*Lord, while there is still time, please provide imaginative
ways in which we can speak forth Your Word of Truth
to all those whom we love. We are grateful that You will
never leave us or forsake us (Hebrews 13:5).*

Some Will be Singing

*"And they sang the song of Moses the bond-servant
of God and the song of the Lamb, saying,
'Great and marvelous are Your works, O Lord God,
the Almighty; righteous and true are Your ways,
King of the nations.'"*
REVELATION 15:3

Those who are victorious over the adversities of the last days on earth will have much to celebrate. This victorious number will include many Jews who come to believe in Christ as their Messiah. And in true Isrealite fashion, they will express their jubilation in song, just as King David did. For the covenant God made with His people stands for all time: "He has sent redemption to His people; He has ordained His covenant forever; Holy and awesome is His name. The fear of the LORD is the beginning of wisdom; a good understanding have all those who do His commandments; His praise endures forever" (Psalm 111:9–11).

Occasionally, I attend Sabbath worship services with a nearby Messianic congregation, for they truly know how to celebrate. Their joyful music resounds as they sing praises extolling the attributes of their faithful God. And this represents only a minute glimpse of the glorious sounds to come, when they will someday worship the Lamb in heaven.

Lord, You alone are worthy of our worship. I praise You with all my heart, and look forward to the day when I will worship You in heaven.